D0031728

The Rape and Recovery of Emily Dickinson

THE RAPE AND RECOVERY OF EMILY DICKINSON

In Her Words
Poems of Witness and Worth

An Autobiography of Emily Dickinson through Her Poems

Marne Carmean

To order additional copies of this book, contact:
Xlibris Corporation
1-888-795-4274
www.Xlibris.com
Orders@Xlibris.com
42511

Contents

Dedicated to

Cathleen Haburton Wells

1945 – 2006

"Never to pass the Angel"

Emily Dickinson

ACKNOWLEDGEMENTS

The author wishes to gratefully acknowledge permission of the publishers and the Trustees of Amherst College to reprint the Dickinson poems (and poem excerpts, first lines), from the following volumes: *The Poems of Emily Dickinson*, Thomas H. Johnson, ed., Cambridge Mass.: The Belknap Press of Harvard University Press, copyright 1951, 1955, 1979, 1983 by the President and Fellows of Harvard College; *The Poems of Emily Dickinson: Variorum Edition*, Ralph W. Franklin, ed., Cambridge, Mass.: The Belknap Press of Harvard University Press, copyright 1998 by the President and Fellows of Harvard College; *The Poems of Emily Dickinson: Reading Edition*, Ralph W. Franklin, ed., Cambridge, Mass.: The Belknap Press of Harvard University Press, copyright 1998, 1999 by the President and Fellows of Harvard College.

Copyright 1890, 1891, 1896 by Roberts Brothers. Copyright 1914, 1918, 1919, 1924, 1929, 1930, 1932, 1935, 1937, 1942 by Martha Dickinson Bianchi. Copyright 1951, 1955 by Alfred Leete Hampson. Copyright 1957, 1958, 1960 by Mary L. Hampson. Originally published in hardcover by Little, Brown and Company, 1960. First paperback edition, 1961.

The author also gratefully acknowledges the following:

The text of the *Dickinson* content from *The Life of Emily Dickinson* by Richard B. Sewall, pp. 19, 20, 24, 41, 50, 59, is reprinted by permission of the publisher, Harvard University Press, Cambridge, Mass. Copyright 1974, 1980 by Richard B. Sewall.

Excerpts from *The Life of Emily Dickinson* by Richard B. Sewall. Copyright © 1974 by Richard B. Sewall. Reprinted by permission of Farrar, Straus and Giroux, LLC.

Excerpts of letters from *The Letters of Emily Dickinson*, Thomas H. Johnson, ed., are reprinted by permission of the publisher, The Belknap Press of Harvard University Press. Copyright 1958, 1986 by the President and Fellows of Harvard College, Cambridge Mass.

Excerpts and scattered quotes from *Emily Dickinson Face to Face*, edited by Martha Dickinson Bianchi, are reprinted by permission of Houghton Mifflin Company. All rights reserved. Copyright renewed in 1960 by Alfred Leete Hampson.

With special thanks to Daryl Sharp, excerpts from *Addiction to Perfection, The Still Unravished Bride* by Marion Woodman, are reprinted by permission of the publisher and general editor Daryl Sharp, Inner City Books, Toronto, Canada. Copyright 1982 by Marion Woodman.

Much thanks to Cynthia Griffin Wolff, for quotes from *Emily Dickinson*. Addison-Wesley Publishing Company, Inc., Copyright 1988, 1986 by Cynthia Griffin Wolff.

Thanks greatly, of course, to Catharine A. MacKinnon, for permission to use her quote from *Only Words*, Harvard University Press, Copyright 1993 by Catharine A. MacKinnon.

The author wishes to gratefully acknowledge the permission of the Trustees of Amherst College to use the Dickinson daguerreotype from the Amherst College Archives and Special Collections.

My thanks to Scarlett R. Huffman: Copyright and Permissions, Harvard University Press.

I would like to state my profound appreciation of Emily Dickinson's biographers, and the authors of the multifarious readings of my bibliography, and beyond, for their scholarship, to thank them for the often steep pleasure I had in reading them.

I would like to state my appreciation also of the Xlibris staff for their courteous expertise and care in the production of this book: Cheryl Gratz, Lynnel Landerito, Niva Costanilla (Author Service Representative), Marco Nepomuceno, Aimee Aborque, Ivan L. Agustin, James Mensidor, Lauro Talibong, Rochelle Mensidor, Anselma Ocon-Cortes and Pam Pasco.

PERSONAL ACKNOWLEDGEMENTS

M y thanks, first and foremost, to my editor, Linda M. DeVore of DeVore & Associates, whose intelligent, diligent attention from the beginning gave my book its middle and end. Deepest thanks to Lois Scott Christensen, friend and editor, who brought a fine point to the final writing, sharpened by Betsy Tice White and Kathryn D'Avanzo. Thanks to the special astuteness of my research assistant, Marie Myers. I wish to give especial thanks to my readers, who over the years offered branches of support, a few themselves poets and writers: the first, Cathleen Wells; among the first, Martin R. Smith, Jerry Stahl, and poets Frank and Peggy Steele; early on, Robert Bly, Kat Ward, Adam Paul, and Corey Bobker. Later, Dr. Margaret D. Evermon, Mollie Martin, and Pamela and Phillippe Mora. At the very last, John Dullaghan, Gloria Goldsmith, David McClure, Robert Reinecke, William Livsey, Joseph Wilkes, and Laura M. Simak. All who by giving of their time and thought gave a coherence and clarity my book could not otherwise have had.

I wish to make my deepest thanks to Robert Brinton Butler, first of friends, for the long and hard work of listening. Then many-leaved thanks to my friends for their helpful interest: Duff Scott, Jay Reiner, Gabrielle R. Crawford, Michael Buscemi, and Jefferson DePeron, as also Lon Price, Tommy Lind, Sal Bernal, and Sheila Jaffe. To Patricia Behr Whitten, Brian Green, Michael Topp, and Henrietta B. Quattrocchi, for their affirmation and friendship of long ago. My aunts Romietta Hawkins and JoAnn Sprague and dear cousin Sharon Isbell Conner were especially sustaining in their encouragement. I wish to thank very much those who in my daily life would ask how my book was coming: Carolyn, Ramon, Mario, Ismael, Maria Ana, Rafat, Brandi, and Katie.

I am grateful to Dr. Catharine A. MacKinnon for her interest and time, and deeply as well, to Dr. Samuel P. Oliner, for the years of both. I wish to thank Dr. Lawrence Lessig for his kindness.

In the making of this book, the lives of my daughters, Siobhan, Helen-Margaret, and Kathlin Carmean, were deeply felt and constant in my contemplations of the fate of gender. I am grateful to my son, Brendahn Carmean, more than he could ever know, for his love and patience. My thoughtful grandson, 'Skylark', Airman First Class, Joseph Schermetzler, is to be named here, honoring his service in Iraq.

In memoriam, Anne Kennedy and Linda A. Weider, whose spirits of intellect and beauty always abide as muses in my life and work.

Preface

644

You left me – Sire – two Legacies –
A Legacy of Love
A Heavenly Father would suffice
Had He the offer of –

You left me Boundaries of Pain –
Capacious as the Sea –
Between Eternity and Time –
Your Consciousness – and Me –
c. 1862

Regarding Edward Dickinson's unholy usurpation of the life of his daughter, premier American poet Emily Dickinson—[1123]*"A great Hope fell"—what force of suppression, devices of almost glacial permanency, could have been so lasting, so intricate, to deny even the possibility of the truth spoken by the poet of an incestuous relationship with her father. Deny and keep hidden throughout a continuous, inexhaustible scholarship and, astoundingly, from the poets of the land ([1167]"Alone and in a Circumstance")? What could possibly have worked so effectively to obliterate truth so profoundly through the several major biographies and the eventual two monumental editions of Emily Dickinson's complete poems by Franklin and Johnson.[†]

---

[*]   All numeric references to first lines, according to Thomas H. Johnson's edition, hereafter will be superscripted preceding the poem.

[†]   These were within thirty years of each other, with the Thomas H. Johnson's Harvard University Press edition, The Poems of Emily Dickinson (1955), printed sixty-five years after her posthumous first volume, Poems, was published in November in 1890 by Roberts Bros. for the Christmas season, also possibly in commemoration of the poet's December 10th birthday.

In between these signal publications were those several editions of poetry and biographical materials published from the warring sides of the poet's family: her sister-in-law Susan Dickinson and her brother Austin's lover, Mabel Loomis Todd, her sister Vinnie switching sides, with this imbroglio to be continued for years by their respective daughters. Now, besides the publication of all of her poetry, there is a gargantuan academic literature derived from many fields of study, a rampant miscellany, created outside those substantial divisions of prosody and American poetry, all of which constantly grows.

There is a range of ideas to fit this basically unanswerable question of why no one has brought openly to mind this paternal sexual transgression, so abundantly presented in all its phases in his daughter's poetry. It might appear that the obdurate, wrought quality of Emily Dickinson's diction and the quantity (1,775)[1] of poems caused the poet to be not sufficiently read, either enough of her poems or with enough care, her meaning often relegated to the outposts of the symbolic. The most ponderable idea is the power of patriarchy and its exercise of an existent social taboo that however seems counterintuitive. Does it make sense to not talk about family behavior that is mortally wounding yet goes on all the time?[2] There was a kind of total quashing of the grotesque reality of life behind closed doors (not shut by the poet), which may yet have swirled slowly in rumor during her lifetime and over the years since her death and initial publication of the poems, as intimated in a 1951 publication by a denial in Richard Chase's *Emily Dickinson*: "[Edward Dickinson] was not, certainly, the tyrant and lover-in-disguise he is sometimes assumed to be."[3] Since when was it 'sometimes assumed' that he was? Certainly this assumption was not made in any of the definitive biographies of the following decades or in any other subsequent large and serious literary investigation that I have been made aware of. The poet herself spoke futuristically and directly to this: [1147]"After a hundred years".

In spite of all of the hard thinking represented by the scholarship necessarily employed in these important tasks, this fundamental question not only still looms but also grows. Cynthia Griffin Wolff, for one, in her 1988 study *Emily Dickinson* provides a foreword by R.W.B. Lewis, in which he puts forth an analysis of amazing verity, a nearly histrionic statement:

> [But] the divine opponent limned in the poetry, according to Cynthia Wolff's remarkable but gradually persuasive reckoning, is anything but the protective father. He (and by all means He) is much rather a liar, a betrayer, a killer, a rapist. In the differing metaphors of differing poems, this appalling deity fumbles lasciviously at our souls, sends Death as his agent to shoot us down, scalps or decapitates us.[4]

Yet this description evidently shone not a glimmer upon the author's mind of perhaps an actual personage in the handsome frame of the poet's father.

Further on, Lewis says, "Similarly, the love poetry, Cynthia Wolff points out, derives from the experience not of fulfillment but of separation from the beloved—...."[5] Again, this about a woman who wrote, and no matter about whom, [249]"Wild nights – Wild nights!". In much of the criticism there is an insistence, antithetical to the spirit of the metaphor, which along with its unique precision should always have a little slipperiness, that the "Father" is, must be, the heavenly father, and the "God" not the human father, nor even of the "River gods" of the Connecticut River Valley of her home and ancestors, right down to her father, Edward. The poem [454]"It was given to me by the Gods – " pertains to the poet's birthright.

Even in language derived from her own lexicon, Emily Dickinson expressed unambiguously her feeling that God is love, echoing William Blake's "Energy is eternal delight" (not to mention 1 John 4: 7-8 "Beloved, let us love one another, ... He that loveth not knoweth not God, for God is love.") and that love is deathless—no matter how alloyed—as it was abominably in her life.

809
Unable are the Loved to die
For Love is Immortality,
Nay, it is Deity –

Unable they that love – to die
For Love reforms Vitality
Into Divinity.
c. 1864

In another vein altogether, but likewise despite the allusion to the heavy reality of rape and missing entirely its potential occurrence, is Marion Woodman's *Addiction to Perfection, The Still Unravished Bride, A Psychological Study*. A Jungian theorist, her ideas in the chapter "Rape and the Demon Lover" are not intended to be given flesh by any specific behavior, yet this statement could not be more apt in its description of Emily Dickinson's experience, in her waking life written in her poetry:

> The father's daughter walks a tightrope above an abyss, putting one foot carefully ahead of the other in a precarious balance between not living at all and living in a highly charged spiritual world.[6]

761
From Blank to Blank –
A Threadless Way
I pushed Mechanic feet –
To stop – or perish – or advance –
Alike indifferent –

If end I gained
It ends beyond
Indefinite disclosed –
I shut my eyes – and groped as well
'Twas lighter – to be Blind –
c. 1863

875
I stepped from Plank to Plank
A slow and cautious way
The Stars about my Head I felt
About my Feet the Sea.

I knew not but the next
Would be my final inch –
This gave me that precarious Gait
Some call Experience.
c. 1864

Woodman's entire chapter is apropos of the life of this unequal, dreadful relationship with a "father-lover complex,"[7] and the "father-god,"[8] Edward Dickinson. To put a point on this, she goes on to say, naming Emily Dickinson and other women writers (Emily Bronte, Virginia Woolf, and Sylvia Plath) as subjects:

> Where the demon lover is the controlling complex in the psyche, the counterbalancing poles of love and loss are both present . . . . The ego has undergone psychological rape, overpowered by the contents of the unconscious.[9]

It is in this passage that, reiterating Lewis in his foreword to the Wolff biography, she illustrates her concept, quoting from an Emily Dickinson poem, [315]"He fumbles at your Soul". And finally, Woodman proffers her learned prescription of simple wisdom:

> Through consciousness a woman may find she can protect herself from the rape of the masculine power principle. To do so she has to remain true to her own feelings, however insecure they may be . . . . The feminine ego can be terrorized by the masculine invasion and its only defense is its authentic feeling.[10]

This was precisely the predicament, and what, perforce, Emily Dickinson enacted repeatedly in her poems, their shell-like structure providing a crucial respite so she could then respond with this saving formula. Truth of feeling sustains the fragile structure—woman or poem—and the moment of transcendence lives on, as did its bearer. This is why I believe Emily Dickinson's bedroom and the "The Old

Homestead,"[1] an abode still standing in Amherst (where they display in replica a small, finely stitched white dress), is hallowed ground to thousands of visitors.[11] It is what makes possible after my "core interpretation"[12] the Recovery part of this book—all comprising *Poems of Witness and Worth*—and what promulgated my odyssey in the cove of Emily Dickinson's life.

Readers can be assured there is a body of Emily Dickinson poetry that is absolutely separate from those pertaining to Edward Dickinson, that portion resultant of his predatory behavior toward his daughter. The profound pain exposed by certain of her poems is not necessarily produced by the poet's father but by life's own greatest griefs, as described in the monumental [341]"After great pain, a formal feeling comes –". In general I think the rule of thirds applies: poems as those within the book that disclose this relationship; another third belonging to a category of those colored or presenting ideation, produced of this paternal perfidy; then a third of the poetry wholly absent the father.

As faithful to Emily Dickinson as I have been to her meaning consistent with the words given in images and metaphors, there is always the possibility of a complete misinterpretation of certain poems. These are most likely to be found in the Indices and not within the book's narrative. Also, it is important for the reader to know that permission was given to use only a limited number of poems in their entirety, eighty-five, but I am confident that those chosen meet substantially the claim of this book as being in the poet's words. There is free use of first lines, as they serve as titles for Emily Dickinson's poems and cannot be copyrighted, and through their utilization, the poet speaking for herself is only abetted.

Here presented is a reckoning at long last with Edward Dickinson's fine-meshed manipulations, foreclosure on his daughter's future, and a misogyny that has gone unrecognized despite a lifetime of documented decisions derived of his power and mendacity, private and public, the most dire toward women, beginning with his mother. The major biographers of Emily Dickinson for years have esteemed the Honorable Edward Dickinson, if not mostly given obeisance, and have glossed over atrocious facts of his private life, even as they consistently relayed them.

My reading experience of the sudden clarity—seeing Edward Dickinson's role as paramour of his daughter—was as though a plumb line dropped down the center had now "trued up" a poem, and by the serrated ripples of this epiphany, I was mesmerized, as dark outer rings disappeared, returning to the mystery of their watery origins, impelling me to read on. A candlepower reading, line by line, of *The Poems of Emily Dickinson*, verified what I believed she was saying

---

[1] I have followed Sewall's designation of the Dickinson residence as "The Old Homestead", based on a congratulatory announcement by the *Hampshire and Franklin Express* when Edward Dickinson repurchased it in 1855.

about her father's sexual opportunism. Finally, I was able to view undistorted and distinct the perennial, passionate subjects and topics of this poet—matrimony, the magnitude, effects of pain, being and dying, the passage of time, immortality, love, of this world, and the afterlife ([1637]Is it too late to touch you, Dear?"). I understood the poet's unrelenting self-surveys of motive and striving, ([744]"Remorse – is Memory – awake – ") she being forced on both sides of betrayal, with excruciating concerns involving an existential paradigm, galaxies away from those conceived and cherished in the popular and scholarly imagination. Myself a poet, I wanted to show these poems written by Emily Dickinson as a testament to the abysmal, immoral relationship that engaged her, with her believing from the beginning that idealistic love would ultimately right, if not make sacred, in her stained-glass soul.

I hope that my providing the aid of an index will objectify and help substantiate for the reader the thematic thinking often found throughout her poetry. I have essentially sorted through the hundreds of poems and put together those sharing a word, a meaning (the same or similar), which set up a convincing chorus of images and ideas, all of what Emily Dickinson was saying about the relationship with her father. This quantitative process (which is discussed at greater length in the Indices) came only after selecting the primary poems of Emily Dickinson's disclosures of this liaison, which early on showed the dimensions and development of intriguing patterns and repetitions, a voluminous poetry, and story, having a beginning, an end, and—posthumously—a beyond for the poet. Finally, for me, it was a testament to the poet's life of prolonged, deep pathos, ensuing a belated advocacy.

REALM OF FIRSTS

I

What is possibly unique, perhaps a first, in the annals of any western spiritual literature is to have in a single work the whole of an author's life (1830-1886) and for it to serve as a formal repository for a truth of manifold pain and whose source could have rent the whole with mortification and shame: [925]"Struck, was I, not yet by Lightning – ". Intrepid and numinous, Emily Dickinson's poetry culminates in love outliving life, [549]"That I did always love", beginning with a juvenile Valentine poem ([1]"Oh the Earth was *made* for lovers, . . .", and sustained in breathless synchronicity ([1039]"I heard, as if I had no Ear"). A poetry of mystic ardor, whether describing simple daylight ([812]"A Light exists in Spring") or a life stalled in pain ([281]"'Tis so appalling – it exhilarates – "), and possessing a complexity of ideas as entrancing as butterflies and imagery as enervating as the goblin bee. The poet, in 1862, reached a creative peak at thirty-one years of age ([365]"Dare you see a Soul *at the White Heat?*") and wrote 366 poems—in themselves constituting a book of her life.

All her 1,775 poems in *The Poems of Emily Dickinson* finally appeared in 1955 in a variorum text of three volumes edited by Thomas H. Johnson. It was an historic publication by Belknap Press of Harvard University Press: without the poems' alteration, as she wrote them, untitled, and (which Johnson considered "musical") with her dashes restored.

II

As the wind faring them forth, the Puritans brought a prevailing spirit upon the pine-scented shores of the unknown, and preordained the discerning spiritual devotion of the future poet: "In the beginning was the Word, and the Word was with God, and the Word was God, . . ." borne to their New World by learned passengers, personifying a cargo of collective literacy, for besides a 1215 Magna Carta, the "wilderness libraries" of Homer, Plutarch, Herodotus, Pliny the Elder, and Virgil, bore the seeds of secularism and ultimately the rule of law—the Massachusetts Body of Liberties—deployed in jury trials, and free elections, a precursor of the Bill of Rights and the Fifth Amendment[13].

Beginning in March 1630, seven ships embarked for Massachusetts. The evangelical Gov. John Winthrop sermonized below the masts of the Arbella (named after his wife) "A Model of Christian Charity," leading Christians of the Great Migration over the waters with hymnal exhortations: "We must delight in each other . . . ," "The Lord will be our God . . . ," and "We shall be as a city upon a hill." And by the end of the year, seventeen ships and a thousand more had arrived.[14] Then as the screws were put to the Puritans in England, ten thousand more in 1634 emigrated.[15] Within a scant decade of the Winthrop followers' arrival at Salem (to what was to become the Massachusetts Bay Colony), Harvard by 1636 had been founded, and in 1640, the Bay Psalm Book was printed in Cambridge.[16]

About 1636, the Dickinsons of Lincolnshire (an extension of the English uplands, and the chalk Downs, "So noble and so bare"[17] of Sussex and Wessex) embarked for the New World.[18] "Before that, in England, the stock from which Emily Dickinson came was clear for thirteen generations more."[19] They were among the last Puritans to migrate not to be merely colonists but for the desire of community, as in 1637 the influx ceased.[20] The Dickinsons arrived most likely through Watertown, and after settling in Wethersfield, Connecticut, moved farther westward along an Indian trail into the wilderness of Western Massachusetts, most probably the old Mohawk Indian trail of a continuous settlement of Calvinist community builders in the late 1630s, staying close to the Connecticut River. (The Dickinsons and others could have been wending their way as an even further branching out of one that took place just before them in the same year 1636 by two reverends and a governor from Cambridge—by the "bent of their spirits"—who went on to establish Hartford, Windsor, and Wethersfield, on the Connecticut River.[21])

Nathaniel Dickinson and Ann Gull settled and soldiered in "the broad alluvial fields"[22] of the Connecticut Valley; sons Samuel and Ebenezer fought defensively at Deerfield during Queen Anne's War "In the Dearfield Medow on the last of Febewarey"[23] a massacre, a cold inferno, in the winter of 1704; and grandsons, Nathan and Nathan Jr. fought the Revolutionary War (1775–1781). The blood of war and afterbirth was spilled on fields where both crops and children were raised in and around villages of thatched-roofed saltbox houses. Emily Dickinson's English forbearers first settled in Hadley in 1659, "New England's errand into the wilderness"[24,] and then its easternmost perimeter became Amherst one hundred years later. Nathaniel was the first recorder and one of the first trustees of Hopkins Grammar School of Hadley, presaging great-grandson Samuel Fowler Dickinson's founding of a college in Amherst.[25] For everybody to be able to read the Bible was a Puritan ideal, and in the Dickinson family intended for both men and women.

Only a year after his granddaughter Emily was born, Samuel Fowler was especially adamant in this view in an 1831 speech to the Hampshire, Hampden and Franklin Agricultural Society that "A good husbandman will also *educate well his daughters.*"[26]

From the beginning, her colonial New England family history, the interior one of stamina and vision, was correlative, pivotally, with the birth of this country. From the time the Dickinsons gained the shore and settled to the establishment of Amherst College by the poet's grandfather, Samuel Fowler, the Dickinson family helped create an Atlantic seaboard civilization, which their illustrious child, Emily Dickinson, raised in her solitary poetry to an astonishing, singular cultural apex—an American one.

III

In the sketch of the Dickinsons' religious and social background (bottom heavy socio-economically) of the following chapters and drawing close to the 1830 birth of Emily Dickinson, and beyond, I wish to show the striations of powerful spiritual and psychological influences, especially those of the poet's grandfather Samuel Fowler. One whose dual heritage of dedication and bankruptcy was onerous for son Edward—the weight of which he levied on his little family, wife Emily Norcross and children Austin, Emily, and Lavinia—impinging sacrificially upon daughter Emily's life.

In his two-volume biography *The Life of Emily Dickinson* (1974), Richard Sewall's broad yet brilliant analysis of the Dickinson family history in the first volume (the second beginning with the poet's birth) renders what he calls the "massive traits"[27] of their lineage from the 1630s Great Migration to the poet's lifetime. (With this as a starting point, he received a generous assist from Perry Miller and his classic *The American Puritan.*) The Dickinson men and women were exceptionally long-lived and hardy, having many surviving offspring. Sewall begins with their "sturdy independence"[28] or ethos ("They must be industrious or perish,"[29]), qualities later refined to Puritan particulars by such phrases as "spirit of sublime self-reliance"[30] resounding in the rough-hewn, fiery preachments of the eighteenth century Jonathan Edwards. Sewall spoke more generally of "the peculiar quality of Connecticut Valley Puritanism"[31] and then quintessentially of Emily Dickinson's spiritual quandaries—her nautical vigilance rooted in Puritanism.[32]

Into the 1800s, ("when there was nowhere one looked that didn't see forest until the Illinois prairie,") these traits retained much of their vigor, witnessed by the life of Emily Dickinson's great-grandfather, Nathaniel Jr., who remarried at seventy and lived to be ninety, dying in 1825 only five years before her birth. Her grandfather Samuel Dickinson's "cannot wait to ride"[33] reply as to why he did not take his four-in-hand from home and instead walked the seven miles to Northampton recalls the "'sublime self-reliance,'" of someone conscientious and habitually obedient to a religious edict. However, this self-reliance seen through a psychological prism appears to be a symmetrical pattern of obsession and compulsion, an earnest if not "'industrious'" impatience that seems to have completely degenerated in his son Edward. It was Edward's corrupting impulsiveness (such as removing someone else's infant from a grave in what was to be the Dickinson plot)[34] that was methodically and sexually transmitted to become the core pain upon which his daughter Emily honed the precision of her poems.

Unbraiding these "'massive traits'" reveals the Dickinson ancestral strands of sinewy, ferocious idealism in both the seventeenth and eighteenth centuries, fighting as settlers and colonists, responding ideologically before and after the Revolution and the Enlightenment, and as Calvinists, evolving to be political, principled, and philosophical. These qualities are evident in Nathan Jr.'s protest in Shay's rebellion, in his and his wife Esther's "love of knowledge";[35] and then in 1821 in their son Samuel's dreams of a college in Amherst. Above all, they are fabulously evident in Samuel Fowler Dickinson's progeny, a poet having a stature of feminine spirituality—brilliant, bold—that no one would have ever dared to imagine in their midst.

The force of the Dickinson libidinous drives can, to a fair extent, be viewed early on as manifest in their large families (besides the biological imperative of blessed genes), and possibly in the late-life remarriage of Nathan Jr., and then florid, wretchedly displaced, as demonstrated by grandson Edward Dickinson's paternal deviance, finding some generational rectification in son Austin's adulterous behavior—a consummated affair of the heart with Mabel Loomis Todd—whom then a felicitous fate chose to transcribe poems for Emily Dickinson's first book after her death. (Susan Dickinson, the poet's sister-in-law, apparently through procrastination, wounded and grieving, lost a genuine prerogative as a life-long reader.)[36]

Those primal, self-perpetuating, familial drives of any one Dickinson generation, becoming distended, destructive, and ultimately a matter of character, are doomed by the eighth generation—the end of the Dickinson patriarchal line. The Dickinson independence of generations became insular, coiling tight under Edward Dickinson. Those passions venerable in Samuel Fowler Dickinson are venal in his son Edward. The sins of her fathers are redeemed in the scrupulous magnificence of the poetry of Emily Dickinson.

The content of Emily Dickinson's poems, those many preoccupied with risk taking and large, all-or-nothing gambles, could have been rooted in a collective memory passed down from those skirmishes as colonialists with Queen Anne's forces or that crucial moment of American Revolutionary history when rich and poor alike took risks of a lifetime as traitors to the Crown if they had lost the war. The poet's family history alone could have sufficed for this oft-recurring theme in her poetry: the Dickinsons' emigration, the defense at Deerfield, great-grandfather Nathan Jr.'s brave participation in Shays' Rebellion, and certainly her grandfather Samuel's loss of "The Old Homestead" funding Amherst College.

Sewall tells of a dream sixteen-year-old Emily had, which she wrote about to her brother: "Father had failed & mother said that 'our rye field which she & I planted, was mortgaged to the Seth Nims'."[37] As Nims was a local postman and political opponent of her father, this could be seen as some kind of a weird continuum of her grandfather Samuel's having made a bid to be Amherst's postmaster about twenty years before and losing to someone who was not an opponent but once a political ally. Trying for the second time to get this well-paying position for his son Edward, he lost once more, and being extremely and uncharacteristically retaliatory involving an unrelated money matter, Samuel Dickinson attempted to have the man removed as guardian of his own children.[38] In 1825, this and other measures or maneuvers (one was to sell his recently deceased father's East Street farm, another to exploit the finances of a widowed sister-in-law), all so painful in desperation, were just to stay afloat as he pursued the pledges for the college fund.[39]

This anecdote of the dream remarkably illustrates the power of the imagination asleep, ego sleepwalking, which can marvelously reconstruct significant scenarios belonging to a past not our own and show in the process that the emotional consequences of our impassioned actions can flow down through the generations in labyrinths of the familial unconscious, ([1631]"Oh Future! Thou secreted peace) and the sleeper's dreams ([1467]"A little overflowing word"). Sewall holds that Emily Dickinson had little or no interest in the Dickinson past as it might have related to her own present.[40] Yet this adolescent letter's disclosure shows the contrary to be the case and that these preoccupations found a place in dreams ([13]"Sleep is supposed to be"), as well as repeatedly in her poems.[41] Unless we are to make a distinction between interest and awareness, Sewall contradicts himself on this point.[42] Samuel Fowler's descendants surely could not on their part separate these forms of cogency, jelled as they were with the infinite disappointment of his dreams and losses. Many years later, Austin offered an honorific tribute to his grandfather in an address prepared for a one hundred and fiftieth anniversary celebration at their First Church of Christ in Amherst.[43]

Perhaps it was this family's obtuse single-mindedness as survivor and settler, the self-serving inner strands, however sacrificial, of always needing to make a cause a Dickinson one, such as defending or farming the land, joining Shays' rebellion, or perhaps, especially, Samuel Fowler's founding of Amherst College. Forming a veritable generational funnel of ambition that was to then precipitously devolve and twist in the egomaniacal and private predilections of the poet's father, Edward Dickinson, ([1744]"The joy that has no stem nor core,").

1377
Forbidden Fruit a flavor has
That lawful Orchards mocks –
How luscious lies within the Pod
The Pea that Duty locks –
c. 1876

Rule of Thirds

V

Vision as Anchor

Emily Dickinson's paternal grandparents, Samuel Fowler and Lucretia Gunn Dickinson, were the first Dickinsons to live in the village proper or "green,"[44] rather than the district of Amherst, on Main Street, which was also to be home to the poet's mother and father, Edward and Emily Norcross, and then December 10, 1830, became the birthplace of the poet, Emily Elizabeth Dickinson. Amherst was the heaven and earth of the Dickinson family story, presence and place inextricable, where Emily Dickinson entered immortality.[45]

It was this third Dickinson generation in Amherst, and the first after the Revolution, of the poet's grandfather Samuel Fowler ([680]"Each Life Converges to some Centre – "), that was most responsible for her station in life, enabling the poet to have the time and leisure to write.[46] Squire Dickinson, lawyer, legislator, community leader and orator, spearheaded the founding of a school, making in 1818 a large monetary contribution to jumpstart the funding for Amherst College.[47] He built in 1813 the first brick house in Amherst, hip-roofed, of the Federalist style.[48] Sewall tenderly stated "the work of Squire Fowler's hands was constantly around Emily from infancy on,"[49] forming the outer casements of her world.

VI

Massachusetts, straight as a breadbox on three sides, Shays' rebellion in the four Western Massachusetts counties, beginning in the fall of 1786, prevented the courts from sitting and thus issuing judgments of foreclosure.[50] Samuel Fowler's father, Nathan Dickinson Jr., on August 25, 1787, had feloniously protested

---

against the imprisonment of these war-indebted farmers at the Northampton court, the county seat for Amherst, and "was obliged to take an oath of allegiance, a stately form of being bound over to keep the peace."[51] It was a moral and material conflagration, for those within this tightly knit fray,[52] especially because the environs of the God-haunted ancestry of Western Massachusetts suffered religious constraints.[53] The Doctrine of the Covenant—The Covenant of Works[54]—of perfect obedience, constituted a spiritual goading and devotion seared deep in the Calvinist soul.[55] The uprising of the farmers could have inveighed doubt upon the rustic consciousness and chaffed conscience.

Jonathan Edwards, who was to become the great philosophical theologian, sermonized in the living memory of the fifteen-year-old Nathan Jr. as pastor at Northampton (1725-1750) of the "visible saints"[56] (as was Edward's grandfather, Solomon Stoddard "the pope of the Connecticut Valley"[57]); and the Dickinson family must have been awash in the earliest waves of the Great Awakening in the 1730s, recorded by Edward's *A Faithful Narrative of the Surprising Work of God in the Conversion of Many Hundred Souls in Northampton* (1736).[58] (Nearly a hundred years later during an extended period of revivals, Emily Dickinson was resolute from her student days at Mount Holyoke Female Seminary onward in her resistance to conversion.)

It was in his last years, in 1765, that the Reverend Jonathan Edwards composed a "Covenant of Grace," the *Dissertation Concerning the End for which God Created the World*,"[59] positing that all is grace between God and mankind, a theology that could have consoled those future souls in the wake of Shays' rebellion. What is more Edwards as a theological philosopher, importantly influenced by John Locke (sharing the core premise of Locke's 1689 *An Essay Concerning Human Understanding* that men could experience and think for themselves, phenomenologically, through Newton's prism), might well have in this dissertation upon, "the communication of the infinite fullness of God to the creature," formed an apotheosis for Samuel Fowler's ideal of higher learning—consciousness consecrated—bracing his elevated aim and vision for Amherst College.

VII

The spirit of Dickinson stalwarts, Nathan and Nathan Jr., was galvanized it seems, as they had farmed for almost two centuries in this country and under the new rule of law stood, if so indebted, to have lost their land. Besides their old roots, they needed to set down other stakes, and their offspring were to be the first Dickinsons to cut the tie to the land for higher pursuits by which to progress and prosper: Nathan Jr.'s and Esther's sons, Timothy and Samuel, were the first to matriculate. From Dartmouth, Timothy Dickinson was to steer from the pulpit toward souls, while Samuel Fowler Dickinson, as a lawyer and civic leader in Hampshire County, went straight to the dusty heart of the populace. Additionally, the dénouement of Shays' rebellion for Nathan Jr., for whom taking an oath of allegiance must have seeped humiliation, could have formed a formidable paternal injunction for Samuel, the last-born son, to move the Dickinsons to higher social ground, which he literally did, as the Old Homestead was raised slightly above Main Street.

Samuel, a true child of the Enlightenment, had an altruistic, parochial perspective, lofty with his generous-minded civic beliefs, and intellect propounding a fervent belief in ideas, which was clearly illustrated in his youthful oratory at twenty-two: "In the temperate climes, in which we live, nature seems to have combined her powers, to aggrandize the intellectual world, and to complete the circle of rational enjoyment . . . . And here she has prepared a banquet for reason."[60] Evangelical, intoned on the Fourth of July, 1797, the speech was originally from his own Salutary 1795 Commencement Address at Dartmouth, translated from the Latin, titled *Nature of Civil Government & Manners; Their Mutual Relation & Influence in Society*.[61] (1797, the last year of Washington's presidency, to be succeeded over the next decade, by the Adams and Jefferson presidencies.) Sustained, Samuel Dickinson's pure and youthful enthusiasm also served years later as a heady source of inspiration for the entire populace of Hampshire County to gladly contribute time and materials for the building of Amherst Collegiate Charity Institution for indigent young men.[62]

VIII

By the autumn of 1846 (and the poet sixteen), a new student at Amherst College wrote in his diary, "This village, which is probably to be my home for the next three years, stands upon a hill, almost at the center of a huge amphitheater formed by the hill or mountains which bound the horizon. The prospect is splendid."[63] If Nathan Jr. could have seen this "prospect," he possibly would have ruminated that his family had farmed there for generations, and now here stood an edifice built upon his and wife's Esther Fowler Dickinson's idealism. Their grandchildren, Samuel Dickinson's children, had rancorously viewed it as a real and unstoppable gamble with their inheritance (subject to the utmost ridicule by his next-to-oldest son, William, and Edward, the oldest,[64]) and it seems, seen as idealistic at its quixotic worst by others outside the family, and by the time he left Amherst for good in 1833, a gamble he had indeed lost.[65]

Samuel's lonely doggedness was a starless, low-slung arc of perseverance, but which apparently he believed was as important for his vision of higher learning for the desiring and deserving, as were gifts of money, (his own alma mater Dartmouth had been founded for the education of the Indian and indigent white male,) a vision which [848]"Just as He spoke it from his Hands" seems to be about. Although the establishment and growth of Amherst College ultimately provided in perpetuity a social anchor for the Dickinson family, it was no mere exercise of ego and enterprise.[66] Perhaps for this his granddaughter wrote as well, [406]"Some – Work for Immortality – ".

An institution, no less, to fortuitously become home to a pioneer astronomer (an observatory was built in 1847), David Todd, whose wife, the gifted Mabel Loomis Todd, later fell in love with Samuel's married grandson Austin Dickinson, and "Caught by beauty,"[67] bent to the arduous task of transcribing the other heavens of Austin's sister's poems for their first publication.[68]

The image to "complete the circle" in Samuel Fowler's oratory seems likely to have been taken from the natural amphitheater of the Pelham hills and the farther-flung Berkshires described by the young diarist. A lasting, verdant setting, and emblematic, befitting the monumental travail, triumphs, and penultimate tragedy of the remaining days of Samuel's life in Amherst and the Old Homestead, now haunting and empty of echoes for the final one—his faraway April burial at sixty-two, [399]"A House upon the Height – " could allude to this.

Squire Dickinson in 1838, self-exiled and impoverished, moved from Cincinnati and the Lane Seminary with wife Lucretia and their remaining small children to a last job post in northern, Hudson, Ohio—dying perhaps completing his own circle—finding solace in the light and latitude of Amherst. The poem [43]"Could live – *did* live – " also might have commemorated this last journey.[69]

There can be little doubt that Jonathan Edward's Calvinist heritage of the "infinite fullness of God", Emily Dickinson's grandfather's nurturing "powers" of nature "to complete the circle of rational enjoyment." ("And here she has prepared a banquet for reason."), the ever-present "amphitheater" and pulchritude of her surroundings, converged, forming a plush poetic cortex, producing her images of a banquet: food, wine, interlocking intoxication and numbness, satiation and starvation, perimeters and infinity, a celestial, circling, spicy, wheel of desire, distant and consummate. ([1620]"Circumference the Bride of Awe")

IX

Amherst was where Emily Dickinson continued to live all of her life and where for almost fifty-six years she wrote and thought of ordinary and extraordinary events, producing poems of the town itself ([783]"The Birds begun at Four o'clock – "), of life on the Connecticut River and Western Massachusetts ([7]"The feet of people walking home", [1407]"A Field of Stubble, lying sere"), of the Salem witch hunt ([1583]"Witchcraft was hung, in History,") of the French and Indian War ([678]"Wolfe demanded during dying"), and of the American Revolution just passed ([1174]"There's the Battle of Burgoyne – "). A highly personal poet holding aloft unique prisms through which to see afresh people and places under the new rule of law and an increasingly secular world, an Emily Dickinson that produced a poetry she is little known for ([1089]"Myself can read the Telegrams"), of politics and systems ([1082]"Revolution is the Pod") and ([1511]"My country need not change her gown,"), and economics ([771]"None can experience stint"). Poems noting social revolution: of a runaway slave ([554]"The Black Berry – wears a Thorn in his side – "), of the underground railroad ([767]"To offer brave assistance"), and of abolitionists (people stood for hours in a field listening to an orator, such as a Sojourner Truth) ([970]"Color – Caste – Denomination – "). The social tragedy: a suicide ([1062]"He scanned it – staggered – "), alcoholism ([1645]"The Ditch is dear to the Drunken man"), and the death penalty ([1375]"Death warrants are supposed to be"). A poem of ageing and the aged ([1476]"His voice decrepit was with Joy – "), elegies inscribed to housewives ([187]"How many times these low feet staggered – " and [154]"Except to Heaven, she is nought."), émigrés ([1096]"These Strangers, in a foreign World,"), and local tragedy ([933]"Two Travellers perishing in Snow"). Those poems arising in the midst of the "Over soul" of the Transcendentalists lingering by Emerson's poem of the flower Rhodora ("If eyes were made for seeing, then beauty is its own excuse for being"), and Thoreau's undistinguished pond.

Along with Emily Dickinson's own incursions into the worlds of commerce and law, and the newly American culture of Boston, Philadelphia, and Washington, all local society flowed through her father's house and around her.[70] The friends, young tutors, and clerks from Edward Dickinson's law office, the opinions of trades people, berry vendors, and college students, and then visitors for cake and wine were all no doubt regaled by Dickinson family lore.

She honors her ancestors who settled on the Connecticut River ([260]"Read – Sweet – how others – strove – "), and also puts in her poetry those strangers who later encroached there ([736]"Have any like Myself") decrying land development.

There was the raging gash of a Civil War, besides the bloodletting, spirit-letting, promulgated by the Manifest Destiny of the Mexican-American War, contriving a country by killing its first inhabitants, native peoples, and decimating cultures clear to California (almost all of the Indian population in that state was vanquished, if not enslaved). In 1862, the year of the Battle of Shiloh, (so many lost), she created the three hundred sixty-six poems.

Through it all, Emily Dickinson wrote at her Sheraton desk up in her bedroom, while below, ambition stirred by homemaking and history in the making, vaulted this new country into the twentieth century, and as Amherst grew from village to college town, Edward Dickinson brought in the railroad. This world steeped in his daughter's soul often found its way into a poem, faintly or hurriedly, penciled sometimes on a receipt or envelope, perchance with flour on the back of her hand.

X

When Emily Dickinson was born in 1830, her brother Austin was two years old, she a middle child, was three at sister Lavinia's birth, last of the siblings. Her parents, Edward Dickinson and Emily Norcross, married in 1828, (they met when as a militiaman he was decamped at Monson, her village home) and in 1830 moved into a house literally split in two, they living on one side (the eastern half) while father and grandfather, Samuel Dickinson, and his family lived on the other, father and son sharing tenancy until the elder's departure from Amherst in 1833.[71] The poet was ten when the family moved from Main into a home of their own on West Street, today North Pleasant Street. Finally, in 1855, Edward Dickinson repurchased the Old Homestead, where the Dickinsons then lived out their days, but for Austin, who was next door at the Evergreens (the first named house in Amherst which he designed and his father built) with his wife and children.[72] Lavinia, after her poet sister's death and outliving Austin, lived alone in the Old Homestead until her death in 1899.

Emily Dickinson's serious, brief, and primarily scientific education was imbued and complexly bound with the spirit and religiosity of the Trinitarians of Amherst Academy and Amherst College, with Noah Webster and Samuel Fowler Dickinson there at the very beginning (1812–1824). Both institutions were completely enmeshed, sharing professors and lectures and an educational syllabi opining the Divine Law of the constancy of creation and enfolding seasons, the purposeful glory of God, hidden or far, bestowed upon all and to be demonstratively witnessed by diligent and devoted studies.[73] As the distinguished geologist and professor Edward Hitchcock exclaimed at Amherst College, "The wide dominions of natural history, embracing zoology, botany, and mineralogy, the theologian has even found crowded with demonstrations of the Divine Existence and God's Providential care and government,"[74] a belief also held fast by his protégé Mary Lyons, who established Mount Holyoke. Emily Dickinson, as inculcated as she was socially and academically, rode out the Great Revival of 1850 on green waves of defiance, "dreaming, dreaming a golden dream, with eyes all the while wide open,"[75] as extolled in a May letter to her friend Abiah Root, having by then found the golden thread of life's meaning in her poetry.[76]

The Amherst Academy was where the yet-to-bud poet was first schooled and then at Mount Holyoke from September 1847 to the following mid May, (the daguerreotype in the Amherst College special collections is of her at this time at seventeen,) when she was withdrawn, not to return, the first known significant reeling in by Edward Dickinson of his daughter. At this point is when the poet began her excuse making to not do the daily social rounds.[77]

Nevertheless, with the exception of not going abroad, it could be said that in the first half of her life, the poet was well traveled in her day. From twelve years of age, Emily Dickinson went to Boston numerous times to visit maternal aunts and cousins, to sightsee, and to obtain homeopathic medicines for a cough that threatened consumption.[78] She also visited Baltimore and a cousin in Middletown, Connecticut, then close to home, Springfield, where Samuel Bowles, editor of *The Springfield Republican* resided, as well as her friends the Hollands.[79] In 1855, after three weeks in Washington, D.C., she and her sister and father (then a member of Congress) continued to Philadelphia, where the poet first encountered the Reverend Charles Wadsworth, probably from the pulpit.[80] This was the deepest of the spiritual bonds and friendships the poet had over her lifetime with several male friends. Two others were the beloved Samuel Bowles, and Henry Vaughn Emmons, author of the essay "Poetry the Voice of Sorrow."[81] With the Reverend, she formed a kinship with a man who by his own admission declared, "My life is full of dark secrets"[82] and who was described by the poet as "my closest earthly friend,"[83] and "He was my Shepherd from 'Little Girl'hood",[84] a special confidant, and they maintained a correspondence until his death, despite his antagonistic relationship with poetry,—"Religious Glorying". Wadsworth was enamored by the mechanical, and prescient, considering the appearance in 1901 of *The Virgin and the Dynamo* by Henry Adams[85].

Peripherally and powerfully, there was Thomas Wentworth Higginson, an important personage in the literary world whom the poet enrolled in her life and who was key to her writing progress and posthumous publication.

Customary and convenient letter writing was a perfect vehicle for Emily Dickinson to stay closely if not intimately connected with those she loved and cared about, expressing with great esprit and acuity what she would perhaps do prudently or reluctantly in person (whether Higginson, Wadsworth, later Judge Lord, or the sundry correspondents of friends and family), and eventually not at all socially, [1639]"A Letter is a joy of Earth – ". Then further, to eternally seal this reticence, Lavinia burned all of her sister's letters after her death.[86]

XI

The Civil War years between 1860 and 1865 seem to have been pivotal in the direction Emily Dickinson was to take from an outer to the inner life of the Old Homestead. A relatively brief span, these years could have predisposed the poet to living an interior life, when having an eye ailment, most likely anterior uveitis, could have shown her the ability she had to live indoors; and living with the fear of blindness possibly accentuated this inward course.[87] Being light sensitive, she wrote her cousin about avoiding glare, "The snow light offends them, and the house is bright . . . ,"[88] a time when the poet might have believed she was caught in life's bellows, as this was just before 1862, the year she created the 366 poems of mind-boggling brilliance, ([272]"I breathed enough to take the Trick – ".)

On April 15, 1862, was when she first wrote to Thomas Wentworth Higginson, editor of *The Atlantic Monthly*, asking, "Mr. Higginson, Are you too deeply occupied to say if my Verse is alive?"[89] It was a period all the more intriguing—homebound and in Boston—when it meant venturing on her own to obtain treatment for ailing eyes with extended stays in Cambridgeport two years in a row from April to fall, 1864 and 1865.[90] Perhaps impaired vision fortified the real permanency of her dependent status, and perambulations in the wider world possibly fully displayed the reality of an overriding, and certainly irrevocable circumstance—the poet turning thirty in the household of her father and decidedly unmarried.

It is through this hidden passage of the Old Homestead that an industry, both academic and publishing, has had the purchase on our collective imagination surrounding the poet's withdrawal behind its doors. Sister Lavinia stated that this was a gradual thing, "only a happen,"[91] and what may have earlier been in part a ruse, protective of her, about providing for the needs of their mother's care.[92] Lavinia might too have added, that this was the point at which the poet became middle-aged, with the most observable single step back at their father's funeral. Held in an overflowing Old Homestead, with the poet staying upstairs (to the great puzzlement of her little niece Martha), Emily Dickinson thus commenced the real reclusion for the remainder of her life. It is said she never visited his nearby gravesite.

The solitude of the last twelve years of the poet's life deepened at intervals as never before—first and most profoundly with the death of her father in 1874—a year later the sweetest depths reserved for the birth of her nephew "Gib," and then her late-life romance with Phil Lord, up until the year 1877—dear friend Samuel Bowles died, and then the dearer Rev. Wadsworth in 1882, and her most recent cherished companion, Judge Lord, in 1884. The Reverend, Judge Lord, beloved nephew Gilbert, and her mother, Emily Norcross, each died within five years of her own death. "[H]ow to repair my shattered ranks is a besetting pain,"[93] she wrote a cousin. At the very last in 1885, fellow poet Helen Hunt Jackson died a year before her own. Emily Dickinson, only "ill since November,"[94] succumbed to Bright's disease on May 15, 1886.

Reign of Pain

XII

"Pain – expands the Time –"

"The Dickinson House is a spacious, center-hall brick home on Main Street about three blocks east of the Amherst village center,"[95] begins Cynthia Griffin Wolff's biography in her prologue, "The Oven Bird,"—where from the Jones Library this scholar could at a befitting distance gaze—at where Emily Dickinson began and ended the story of her life, outliving its great tragedy, gaining the transcendence fought for in her poems, told in [1081]"Superiority to Fate".

Edward Dickinson, a major in the state militia, took to writing "Maj. Dickinson" over the masthead of the newspapers he subscribed to and saved. This bearing of citizen soldier, even when not arrayed in the "sword, sash, and plume"[96] of parade regalia, had a militaristic authority, comportment, imposed upon one and all. Millicent Loomis Todd, a newcomer to Amherst and only a short time later crucial to the Dickinson saga, was moved to say, "No one openly opposed his decisions, least of all his family."[97]

486
I was the slightest in the House –
I took the smallest Room –
At night, my little Lamp, and Book –
And one Geranium –

So stationed I could catch the Mint
That never ceased to fall –
And just my Basket –
Let me think – I'm sure
That this was all –

I never spoke – unless addressed –
And then, 'twas brief and low –
I could not bear to live – aloud –
The Racket shamed me so –

And if it had not been so far –
And any one I knew
Were going – I had often thought
How noteless – I could die –
c. 1862

"I was the slightest in the House – " is from a now-grown poet who sees herself as diminutive, isolated, and static—dependent, poised—to "catch the Mint." Her home life is repressive, where speech is monitored, of proscribed tones, and in the last line, she depicts a house silenced, emulative of death. [770]"I lived on Dread – " takes this subject of the toxicity of the Dickinson home atmosphere to a greater, single-veined depth of fear.

There are two main beliefs about Emily Dickinson's life, one is of the overblown fact of her living life as a recluse her adult entirety; and within the folds of this reclusion is tucked the belief of a "Mystery lover," all in the absence of corporeal fact. The one constant male figure, her father's presence, I knew certainly held taut sway over her life, and it was thinking this when sprang to mind the two well-known poems "Forever at His side to walk –" and "I never lost as much but twice,". It was when I reread these poems that the possibility of her father having had sexual relations with her first occurred to me.

246
Forever at His side to walk –
The smaller of the two!
Brain of His Brain –
Blood of His Blood –
Two lives – One Being – now –

Forever of His fate to taste –
If grief – the largest part –
If joy – to put my piece away
For that beloved Heart –

All life – to know each other –
Whom we can never learn –
And bye and bye – a Change –
Called Heaven –
Rapt Neighborhoods of Men –
Just finding out – what puzzled us –
Without the lexicon!
c. 1861

49
I never lost as much but twice,
And that was in the sod.
Twice have I stood a beggar
Before the door of God!

Angels – twice descending
Reimbursed my store –
Burglar! Banker – Father!
I am poor once more!
c. 1858

    The personages of both poems are certainly the poet and her father. "Brain of His Brain – / Blood of His Blood – " could not be more explicit and self-referential unless when writing "Burglar! Banker! – Father! – ". In her poem's literalness are the intonations of entrapment and betrayal. The "Angels – twice descending" apparently preceding [1732]"My life closed twice before its close – ". Besides sharing a confiding resonance, there are for examination two poems having the same idea—the previous "All life – to know each other – Whom we can never learn – " and in the poem below: "But in Each Other's eyes / An Ignorance beheld – / Diviner than the Childhood's". She sees both of them, each to each, unfathomable to one another, no matter how they engage, as they will always be in their connection father and daughter, roles not to be rationally encompassed.

568
We learned the Whole of Love –
The Alphabet – the Words –
A Chapter – then the Mighty book –
Then – Revelation closed –

But in Each Other's eyes
An Ignorance beheld –
Diviner than the Childhood's –
And each to each, a Child –

Attempted to expound
What Neither – understood –
Alas, that Wisdom is so large –
And Truth – so manifold!
c. 1862

The schoolroom motif of the ABCs and book learning is a setting Emily Dickinson employs often in her poems allegorically, as in [418]"Not in this World to see his face – " and [728]"Let Us play Yesterday – ". In the latter, the encoded meaning is clear (in the fourth stanza, bird-like, not wholly out of her shell, she falls, unable to fly), and this opens up "Not in this World to see his face – ": a God-like father taking her future and freedom for himself—the one of her own she will never know, the other never have.

XIII

The Dickinsons and the greater farming community of the Connecticut River valley gained renown as "The River Gods," a legacy that extended to their lawyer grandson Edward Dickinson.[98] It was an old Romanesque nomenclature that must have seemed to him both antiquated and pleasing, as the pinnacle of his ambition in the mid-nineteenth century was to bring the railroad home. A success that prompted his daughter to write of the Amherst & Belchertown Rail Road, a branch line completed June 1853, [585]"I like to see it lap the Miles –".

Samuel Fowler Dickinson left Amherst with the youngest children and wife Lucretia Gunn for good on December 16, 1833, which prompted Edward Dickinson soon after to confide to his father-in-law, "I have always thought that such a change in relation to my father would prove for my advantage here and be an additional reason for remaining,"[99] as soon would be an economic boom for Western Massachusetts of the mid-1830s, and as far as his ethics (to be proven flaccid) would allow.[100]

What had been exhilarating hope for the Dickinsons turned to a desolate bankruptcy in one generation—Samuel's loss of home and heart—countervailed by the resentment and rage of his son. Edward Dickinson enacted a deep-seated, quiet unscrupulousness throughout his business life, expressed in underhanded decisions and deeds, and was even surprisingly chaotic in his record-keeping duties as treasurer of the college.[101]

Being a descendant of the "River Gods" suited the grandiose notion of who Edward thought he was, securing a well-tended Dickinson persona, as did his jet and diamond stickpin, detail a solid delusional basis for the self-made man he fancied himself to be. Edward picked up exactly where his father left off in Amherst's civic and collegiate life. Self-serving and devoid of risk, he immediately set about perpetuating the tradition of civitas to which his father had dedicated himself for forty years. He was first the town clerk as his father had been, in a very few years, and again as his father, he became treasurer of the college for the next several decades. The one role he did not assume was that of Deacon, the charitable arm of the Dickinsons' church, which Samuel had been for decades. Unlike the elder Dickinson, Edward achieved all this without any of the duress of dedication, and again, unlike his father, he was able to finagle a life-long prosperous law partnership with his son Austin, who was next in line to carry on the duties of Amherst college treasurer.

Edward Dickinson came into his own as the new monetary capitalism of the Industrial Revolution was insinuating itself with "merchants whose capital enabled them to control the supply of raw materials and the marketing of the finished products,"[102] producing an economic consciousness that Dickinson wanted to lay in preparation for and which he did, much to his great personal advantage. He almost doubled his net worth between 1866 and 1868 in local land acquisition (most importantly getting back his father's house), manufacturing, bringing in the railroad, and helping establish Massachusetts Agricultural College.[103] The one personal and salient, beneficent, move by Edward Dickinson was the repurchase of the family home so that his wife and daughters had a place to live out their years.[104] His need to hold onto power made unwieldy a common but vital family matter—to draw up a will—this inability at the end left an estate to Austin to divide, which he never did while keeping both households going as one.[105]

730
Defrauded I a Butterfly –
The lawful Heir – for Thee –
c. 1863

Edward was inordinately preoccupied with all things social, show and accoutrements, besides being determined to exploit the Dickinson name for the monetary resuscitation of a River God, while his daughter Emily, who lauded the democratic Daisy ([285]"The Robin's my Criterion for Tune – "), duly marked it in her poetry. There are many poems pre-occupied with wealth, in the loss, accrual, or appearance of it, their own Western Massachusetts affluence—endless ruminations of circumstance and means—often reverting in reference to her economic powerlessness. Or, as disclosed in her poem [299]"Your Riches – taught me – Poverty.", she treasures penury as long as she has a life with him.

XIV

Edward Dickinson's vain egotism is depicted almost satirically by granddaughter Martha Dickinson Bianchi in her memoir, *Emily Dickinson Face to Face: Unpublished Letters with Notes and Reminiscences.*

> For even though the Squire passed down an empty street, by the Sweetser's cow pasture on his left and reached no habitation until his son Austin's, the silk hat and gold cane were the indispensable adjuncts of his like in the eighteen-sixties.[106]

Emily made mockery of Dickinson's sartorial pretensions in an 1850 letter to Austin: "Father looks very grand, and carries his hands in his pockets in case he should meet a *Northampton man.*"[107]

It appears that from this same grandiosity of Edward Dickinson fell a possessive power, coveting his daughter, underlying the writing of this letter to her at only eight years of age: "Be pleasant to your little brother & sister, help all get along as pleasantly as you can. I want to have you one of the best little girls in town."[108] By this means making her pre-eminent in his attention, he is already positioning her to meet his needs, poised for leverage, putting her first, and implying that she is in charge of an older brother and a younger sister. (The demand "best little girl" was quoted years later in a "Master" letter.[109]) With cunning, Edward Dickinson discerned a daughter's devotion that could provide the blind behind which he could subvert innocence—to manipulate, fondle a filial trust, ([6]"Frequently the woods are pink –").

Perhaps it was grandfather Samuel Fowler's exalted sense of mission, stymied, and mortified, that carried over in Edward, his first-born son, as a massive and misaligned impulse, converting into a carnal force of monstrous individuation, exposited by his daughter in [23]"I had a guinea golden –". The poet plainly describes herself as sullied in the heart-breaking poem [428]"Taking up the fair Ideal," and further indicts her father's harming of her with [877]"Each Scar I'll keep for Him", (*he* cries for her) and where in the last line the poet adopts a childlike articulation, a way of expressing that a child is the true victim of adult debauchery.

It may have been that the poet's joyous consciousness as a child described in the first stanza of [869] "Because the Bee may blameless hum" and in the second, trusting as a flower, is what brought Edward Dickinson's erotic focus upon her little person, irrepressible, and freckled, in [1094]"Themself are all I have – ". The last stanza of [70] ""Arcturus" is his other name –" describes a father's specific behavior and a self-description involving an aspect of behavior, both evocative of first hand experience.

XV

"The Face we choose to miss – "

The most telling objective detail Emily Dickinson gave in all her poetry of this relationship belongs, not surprisingly, to the physical features, the facial ones, their distinctive dimples and eyes. (The dimples were a major feature of her own physical identity, [351]"I felt my life with both my hands" and her father's [1529]"'Tis Seasons since the Dimpled War".) In [939]"What I see not, I better see – " the poet gives us the color of her eyes (at least that color she chose for her poetry), which shows up significantly again—sharing this resemblance of her father's eyes—depicted in "Joy to have merited the pain – ".

788
Joy to have merited the Pain –
To merit the Release –
Joy to have perished every step –
To Compass Paradise –

Pardon – to look upon thy face –
With these old fashioned Eyes –
Better than new – could be – for that –
Though bought in Paradise –

Because they looked on thee before –
And thou hast looked on them –
Prove Me – My Hazel Witnesses
The features are the same –

So fleet thou wert, when present –
So infinite – when gone –
An Orient's Apparition –
Remanded of the Morn –

The Height I recollect –
'Twas even with the Hills –
The Depth upon my Soul was notched –
As Floods – on Whites of Wheels –

———

To Haunt – till Time have dropped
His last Decade away,
And Haunting actualize – to last
At least – Eternity –
c. 1863

The eyes and facial resemblance are corroborated in two books by her niece Martha Dickinson Bianchi, who lived next door to her Aunt Emily and grandfather Edward Dickinson. In *The Life and Letters of Emily Dickinson*, Bianchi notes, "His hair was a dark auburn, and his eyes those that Emily repeated in time."[110] (The poet reveals [32]"When Roses cease to bloom, Sir," her hand prefers resting in auburn, presumably, hair.) In *Face to Face*, "His daughter Emily reproduced him in more than coloring of the hair of red bronze, the wine-brown eyes that could flash with indignation or soften in approval, that were common to them both."[111] This likeness is obvious especially in the paintings (family portraits by Otis A. Bullard when Emily was ten) and reproduced by the very few photographs that were made of the Dickinsons.

In the following poem, the poet compares their physical likeness using a general physical description with "We Two – looked so alike – " and pleads "'Twas love – not me – ", it was love, not will, and states woefully, "Such Guilt – to love Thee – most!" then she defends loving him as no worse than Jesus loving humanity. (An identification with Jesus she clearly conveys in [1487]"The Savior must have been".) The poet makes a flat declaration of their filial resemblance, further imploring "Justice" to see correctly that "We Two – looked so alike – ". It was in this way they were helplessly guilty, and not of loving one another.

394
'Twas Love – not me –
Oh punish – pray –
The Real one died for Thee –
Just Him – not me –

Such Guilt – to love Thee – most!
Doom it beyond the Rest –
Forgive it – last –
'Twas base as Jesus – most!

Let Justice not mistake –
We Two – looked so alike –
Which was the Guilty Sake –
'Twas Love's – Now Strike!
c. 1862

[336]"The face I carry with me – last – " is a poem in which she points out to an angel interlocutor that her worldly significance, personhood, was in the physical likeness she bore to her father and by having his name.

The line "Savior, I've seen the face – before!" from a poem that comes later in the chapter "In the House" seems forthright when first read, but then reading it again, could be a mirror image—seeing in her father—herself.

A Gnostic tone and inflection, of many lines, even stanzas, involving numerous poems connotes a story whose verity is dependent on a belief based solely on the truth-telling of the witness, as it cannot be seen or proved. Probably her sacrifice—life, body—and crucifixal pain was in the poet's purview as great as Jesus': [553]"One Crucifixion is recorded – only – " or in the fourth stanza in [1737]"Rearrange a "Wife's" affection!", where the poet refers to the crown of thorns she wore every day. There is a self-defining poem using the persona of Jesus, [488]"Myself was formed – a Carpenter – ". Again, descriptively and daringly she compares herself to Jesus in the quality of love for her father ([833]"Perhaps you think me stooping").

Jesus' love toward God the Father most likely afforded a precise and objective gauge of her devotion toward Edward Dickinson. [1736]"Proud of my broken heart, since thou didst break it," is a poem of unusually long lines, where the poet creates blatant parallels of feeling, joyous fathoms, and suffering so akin to Jesus' that she appropriates as imagery His cross as her own. [85]"They have not chosen me," he said," is about the lack of reciprocity in the relationship, again paralleling the relationship Jesus had with humanity, becoming persecutory, qualitatively conveying the agonizing aspect of her pain.

456
So well that I can live without –
I love thee – then How well is that?
As well as Jesus?
Prove it me
That He – loved Men –
As I – love thee –
c. 1862

Then a lament, hyperventilated, begins with the line [217]"Savior! I've no one else to tell – ". Her niece notes in *Face to Face*, "I have seen her face stern, as if in judgment of her own soul or fate. She looked like my grandfather then—trying the Providence above her, perhaps, before her own tribunal,"[112] a quality that is illustrated in her poem [1461]""Heavenly Father'" – take to thee" and appears subtlety so in [497]"He strained my faith – ", besides it seems in these Emily Dickinson conducted a colloquy with herself. [62]"Sown in dishonor"! the poet ends in a touching wish for forgiveness in [237]"I think just how my shape will rise – " and [502]"At least – to pray – is left – is left – ".

XVI

Emily Dickinson does not need corroboration in her poetry—either you hear her or you don't. However, in the wake of the unsettling revelation of the nature of this father-daughter relationship ([434]"To love thee Year by Year – "), I had a need to go to the poet's major biographers, desiring to find confirmation of my reading within the context of the character and circumstance of the Dickinson family. Richard B. Sewall's *The Life of Emily Dickinson* (1974) was the first definitive biography, beginning its second volume at the poet's birth; and I reread an early (1938) pioneering, affectionate survey by George Frisbie Whicher, *This Was a Poet: A Critical Biography of Emily Dickinson*. In Cynthia Griffin Wolff's *Emily Dickinson* (1988), the symptomology is replete of a long-suffering family in an incisive family history both scholarly and psychologically astute. (The little over a hundred pages she devotes to her chapter "My Father's House" could be a careful and cogent case study given to the therapeutic models of family systems theory.) The last to be read was Alfred Habegger's fairly recent, extravagantly researched *My Wars Are Laid Away in Books* (2001).

XVII

The "compact village"[113] of Amherst was once described as having structures painted in yellow and white, wooden, with shutters, "a neat and pretty place,"[114] and was becoming by mid-century one of the many little dawns of the Industrial Revolution.

The Edward Dickinson family, modern and nuclear in the absence of an extended family member, was a self-sustaining household of five. (Lucretia Gunn returning from Ohio a widow faced being made effectively homeless disallowed from her son Edward's home.) Their family pain was to an extent a legacy of her husband, Samuel Fowler, because of Edward's obsession with gaining repossession of the property and prestige his father had sacrificed for the College. Far exceeding that was Edward Dickinson's soul-destroying obsession that enveloped the body and being of his daughter. He was an autocrat whose own agenda of control was paramount, presiding over a family of covert relationships and chronic unhappiness.

For Emily Norcross Dickinson, it seems the nadir of this matrimonial union was when her husband purchased back the Old Homestead, returning to where she had lived early in her marriage, and then suffered a "collapse"[115] resulting in a long period of depression and invalidism. A moment of family gravity possibly delineated in [965]"Denial – is the only fact".

At the outset for Emily Dickinson, the choice to be born her father's daughter was, of course, not hers, nor was his sexualization of her, ("Baptized – this Day – a Bride"). Probably long before adolescence, Emily knew that she had a special relationship with her father; from a child's perspective it had always been so, as eldest daughter would always be so. Meanwhile, Edward Dickinson had by her childhood already co-opted her sense of self-worth ([603]"He found my Being – set it up – " and [1462]"We knew not that we were to live – "). Even before his laying a hand on her—to literally do so—believing herself lovable was entirely in his hands. ([427]"I'll clutch – and clutch – " where she is alternately anxious and appeasing).

Edward reckoned early on that if his poet daughter, also named Emily, was given a chief position in the household, it would keep her where he wanted her ([1072]"Title divine – is mine!"). Beloved brother Austin had a singular standing as firstborn and only son, and a loyal younger sister, Lavinia, being practical, deferred, sensing a powerful familial agenda: remarkably in a poem titled *Night* she wrote "The stars kept winking and blinking, / as if they had secrets to tell; / But as nobody asked any questions, / Nobody heard any tales."[116]

The poet gaining dominance in the household can be ferreted out: a fundamental desire, naturally, to be for her father "the best little girl in town", and locked in this way, she was set up by Edward, juxtaposed, against her mother's nature and personality, so disparate from her own, ([220]"Could *I* – then – shut the door – "). The opposite, presumed deeply opposing, personalities of the two Emilys could have enabled a dynamic of a silent rupture between an acquiescent Emily Norcross Dickinson, and impassioned, intellectual daughter [1219]"Now I knew I lost her – " cynically set in motion by the imperious husband and father.

It seems inevitable this mother-daughter bond would have an alienating disharmony (if not dissonance) perhaps neurobiological, of differing qualities: the poet dominant, sharp, and subtle, while Mrs. Dickinson, was "timid of mistakes,"[117] and vague, although the poem [1085]"If Nature smiles – the Mother must" connotes she could perceive her family accurately. A soft-featured, sweet-faced woman, as can be seen in the Bullard portrait, known in the small Amherst for her "cruellers and custards"[118] and unrelenting hospitableness[119]. She was a depressive, periodically invalid, alternately taking waking refuge in her self-absorption or wresting control in an obsession with household cleanliness.[120] Throughout her marriage Mrs. Dickinson was not within the purview of family politics as someone who mattered.[121] As Edward Dickinson's wife, "She trembled and flustered, obeyed and was silent before him,"[122] and excluded from family business affairs, enough to forge her signature.[123] Daughter Emily, from the age of thirteen to thirty-three, was the sole signatory as witness on thirteen of twenty-one known legal documents (mainly her parents' sale of property), with the remainder witnessed by Austin and Lavinia.[124] She is never mentioned in her daughter-in-law Susan Dickinson's years of letter writing.[125]

For nineteen years Emily Norcross alone in the family was "saved," and her Christian devotion as a mother and wife, compartmentalized, must have been continually buffeted, (as was her avoidance) by unmanageable and unimaginable forces; but, she could have been much less deluded than one might believe, [164]"Mama never forgets her birds,".[126] Perhaps she felt supplanted, because according to grandchild Martha, "To them both, father and daughter, inner lives were solemn and private things,"[127] and "their unspoken intimacy went so deep it never came to the surface in words, but was never absent, diminished, or lost or ceased to be."[128] Who knows what this Emily Norcross did or did not know, as [859]"A doubt if it be Us" infers; as does, after her stroke, Mrs. Dickinson was unable to understand how Emily could go to bed and not wait up for him. (In a later chapter, "In the House", the candid [368]"How sick – to wait – in any place – but thine – " depicts a routine which would have functioned as a pertinent reality check for Mrs. Dickinson.)

In the genetics of tragedy, she may have been the tragic one in the Dickinson family, for it was said of her father Joel Norcross in his small Monson community "many hated him heartily while he lived."[129] And then to have as husband the concupiscent Edward Dickinson, his life pleated with hidden agendas. For her husband, it was rather all power and all for his pleasure, [1196]"To make Routine a Stimulus". Mrs. Dickinson suffered an incapacitating stroke in 1875, a year after her husband's death. About her reaction to Edward Dickinson's demise, Cynthia Wolff writes, "her shock and grief are scarcely mentioned in any accounts of the family's history."[130] According to Habegger, Samuel Bowles sent a box of flowers for her first Thanksgiving as a widow, and one year it was thankfully noted she didn't cry much. In the end she was given great succor by the ministrations of her daughters, and especially from Emily.

XVIII

Those who are victims of incest cope variously with the protracted trauma of ongoing sexual opportunism and oppression, usually by a father ([1462]"We knew not that we were to live – "). One way is to be reciprocal, or to seem so, even especially to oneself ([374]"I went to Heaven – "). To "love" the perpetrator back feels less contorted, painful, the incongruity lessened, as I believe was the case with Emily Dickinson. However, rather than feel self-condemnation solely ([256]"If I'm lost – now"), the poet commits to live ([677]"To be alive – is Power – ") and to love ([549]"That I did always love"). Even girding this cognitive dissonance of global magnitude ([1727]"If ever the lid gets off my head"), which results in a terminus of self-obsession created of wit and woe in [642]"Me from Myself – to banish – ".

A few of the "Bride" poems create an impression that the poet-daughter was almost elevated to surrogate wife by Edward's merely giving the word; but by withholding it, he seems to have reneged. And thus was created, I believe, the powerful, and lethal vortex of the "Bride" poems—her [1737]"Rearrange a "Wife's" affection!". The obsessive focus on her own status in the household to be "wife" appears to be what the poet saw as a means to gain a control in a spasmodic relationship. Bereft of this, it was being true to him, as told by *two* messengers, not only to the very end of the world, but again to rededicate herself, sterling, indispensable, even as the heavens dispersed ([400]"A Tongue – to tell Him I am true!"). Cynthia Wolff mistakenly tilted it to be daughter Emily's emotional neediness draining Edward Dickinson.[131] Yet it was she who was left with [959]"A loss of something ever felt I – " in which plaintive, and retrospective, never fitting in, she ruminates about where she belongs, wonders if looking about and down rather than up is a mistake.

She desired a legitimization of this relationship—sanctification as a painkiller—perhaps even the baking of breakfast loaves for him, leading her to imaginatively conjecture, [944]"I learned – at least – what Home could be – " and at times believe it true in her case.[132] Her love would be justified in matrimony, an idea plain as day in the last line of [322]"There came a Day at Summer's full,". In another poem relevant to this belief, Emily Dickinson makes a unique projection into motherhood with a hundred cradles abloom: [133]"As children bid the Guest "Good Night".

732
She rose to His Requirement – dropt
The Playthings of Her Life
To take the honorable Work
Of Woman, and of Wife –

If ought She missed in Her new Day,
Of Amplitude, or Awe –
Or first Prospective – Or the Gold
In using, wear away,

It lay unmentioned – as the Sea
Develop Pearl, and Weed,
But only to Himself – be known
The Fathoms they abide –
c. 1863

XIX

It is in the historic protection of the image of the good, if not ideal, father, buffed by the regard of an always-deferential biographer, that Emily Dickinson's fate at his hands—the forbidding, escalating possessiveness of Edward Dickinson—has mainly been disguised, while she remains forever trapped in the amber guise of the recluse poet.

273
He put the Belt around my life –
I heard the Buckle snap –
And turned away, imperial,
My Lifetime folding up –
Deliberate, as a Duke would do
A Kingdom's Title Deed –
Henceforth, a Dedicated sort –
A Member of the Cloud.

Yet not too far to come at call –
And do the little Toils
That make the Circuit of the Rest –
And deal occasional smiles
To lives that stoop to notice mine –
And kindly ask it in –
Whose invitation, know you not
For Whom I must decline?
c. 1861

Between "recluse" and "poet" there is the real-world truth of her hidden in the glades of solitude, as stated above in "Henceforth, a Dedicated sort – / A member of the Cloud." However, it is clear in this poem that the line "My Lifetime folding up –" is about Edward Dickinson's actions, "Deliberate as a Duke would do", and if she was to have a life to call her own, it would have to be as "a Dedicated sort . . . A Member of the Cloud." Distinguishing herself from a dilettante, this same image and meaning would be rendered again in the line "My Business, with the Cloud," perhaps like those of Socrates: "And to commune and talk with our own deities the Clouds"; or as described by Aristophanes, "Shining tempters formed of air, symbols of desire;" of the enchanted poet.

Emily Dickinson's reluctance (contradistinct desire) to publish, even as she sought validation from Thomas Wentworth Higginson, the literary editor of *The Atlantic Monthly*, was simply that she did not want to draw attention to herself publicly, even as editor-in-chief Thomas Niles (*A Masque of Poets*) solicited her work.[133] The Higginson correspondence, after the first, never again bore the Amherst postmark, as presumably her handwriting could have been recognized by Boltwood the postmaster.[134] She once paled "so white"[135] when a poem of hers, published anonymously, was recognized by Susan Dickinson that she regretted having mentioned seeing it. The poet did not want to risk Edward Dickinson's knowledge of her writing life, which he had the power to prohibit, [985]"The Missing All – prevented Me".

Strength of mind clearly safeguarded the precincts her father could not control, because he could not enter her sublime thinking life: [945]"This is a Blossom of the Brain – " [998]"Best Things dwell out of Sight"—nor could he obtain to the gravitas ([1126]"Shall I take thee, the Poet said") or clamber as he might, her plane of intellect, ([1730]"Lethe" in my flower," or [822]"This Consciousness that is aware"). Each of the following poems, pellucid, complex, are all about these processes of thought: [1158]"Best Witchcraft is Geometry", [711]"Strong Draughts of Their Refreshing Minds", [1452]"Your thoughts don't have words every day", [701]"A Thought went up my mind today – ", and [1071]"Perception of an object costs". The profundity of experience proffered intellectual summitry—a volcanic truth ([836]"Truth – is as old as God – " and [1455]"Opinion is a flitting thing,"). Most explicit was the credo, a declaration ([1453]"A Counterfeit – a Plated Person – "), saying that the truth is natural, good, with security and liberty going hand in hand. What are clearly lies will be heard far beyond the grave.

Secret to the Grave

XX

A bias can be much like a reed that holds stalwart above the swiftly flowing water, even as a silt of evidence would show it faulty, if not the opposite as true. Such is the case with Edward Dickinson being an honorable father and husband, as purported uniformly in the biographies of his daughter, not even a man of dark complexity, perhaps only opaque in character, somewhat benighted.[136] This, although there are numerous significant glimpses that consistently reveal sides of him to be quite other than he was customarily perceived by his biographers and give enough cause for the attentive reader to surmise that Edward Dickinson was to be feared not with respect but warily. There are the well-known life-sized portraits of his own making: his militaristic pretensions, the distasteful Coeleb papers, (locally published), proselytizing for the subjugation of women, and his vociferous abhorrence for those who were not kept under a man's thumb.[137]

The entire Edward Dickinson section in Sewall's first volume on Emily Dickinson is so ameliorative in tone and concept as to repair this image of record, if not replace it with propaganda, approbative, and intricately inlaid, writing of a man we would wish him to be other than the one he was. Because there can be found enough material that is dense with authentic detail to view with easy perspicuity the pathology of this man's nature, whether it is public record, archival accounts documented in letters, diaries or interviews, notes of contemporary observation—of the primary sources, surveyed in the notes of his daughter's biographies.

His rage alone, as Vinnie in a letter forewarned brother Austin, "You know home has not altered in your absence & sometimes the *fire kindles suddenly!*",[138] was of an anger that was sociopathic—whether enraged because of a chip in a plate put before him, which his daughter the poet pulverized (it seems Sewall supported the view that it was about family standards and "workmanship"[139]) or beating a horse in his stable because he didn't look "'umble,'"[140] with Emily screaming in the background. Addressing this horrific scene, Sewell provides an advisory in a hefty footnote, a reprint of an open letter in *The Springfield Republican* from Edward Dickinson, of his almost grateful elation to be invited to a banquet by the National Horse Exhibition: "The letter should be read, surely, in conjunction with Vinnie's story of his beating the horse,"[141] which "'conjunction,'" if it showed anything, would be a cruel narcissism. A generation or so later, Alfred Habegger's biography deigned this rage as being protective, hinged on paternal fears of his family's general vulnerability with three dependant women, and tends overall toward a quaint, respectful view of Edward Dickinson. Woolf, also respectful toward the father, foremostly desired an evenhanded approach to her characterization of the Dickinson family members.

Richard Sewall's skewed interpretation began with calling the oppressive Dickinson home life a "legend" begun in later years by a bitter Lavinia,[142] all of which he capped on the last page by declaring, "Emily could have helped him more than she did, a delinquency she realized only after he died."[143] In truth, the shadowy patriarchal Hon. Edward Dickinson enacted a sinister protection of his affairs and family's privacy ([112]"Where bells no more affright the morn – " or as perhaps put forth in [1451]"Whoever disenchants").[144] A covert behavior, whether it was in defiling his daughter, in not leaving a will, or in the shout "'Boy, shut that gate!'"[145] to the residence. It was, as well, clearly calculating, indicated early on as the word "confidences" was interchangeable with "secrets" in his courtship letters to young Emily Norcross.[146]

XXI

Of the 1775 poems Emily Dickinson left behind, saved in a chest of drawers, some in slender packets sewn (it is said, with red yarn) in about a third of the poems she provided herself as witness to her father's rape and abandonment. (Usually there are no witnesses of family sexual abuse, sometimes siblings, seldom to rare a parent.)

It could be that the mass of her poetry offered a global cover to the poems of this relationship, perhaps her own unconscious contribution to keeping the secret for a century [1129]"Tell all the Truth but tell it slant –". Consciously, Emily Dickinson was living in shame, described in the poem [362]"It struck me – every Day –" as lightning from a stationary cloud.

Sapphic, sexually sentient, if not besotted, and auburn, white complexioned, "Her face was in a bed of hair" is a telling self-portrait. The poet boldly asserts, "Who witnesses, believes," testifying that Edward Dickinson had broken the unwritten commandment in the seduction of his daughter.

1722
Her face was in a bed of hair,
Like flowers in a plot –
Her hand was whiter than the sperm
That feeds the sacred light.
Her tongue more tender than the tune
That totters in the leaves –
Who hears may be incredulous,
Who witnesses, believes.
c. ?§

733
The Spirit is the Conscious Ear.
We actually Hear
When We inspect – that's audible –
That is admitted – Here –

For other Services – as Sound –
There hangs a smaller Ear
Outside the Castle – that Contain –
The other – only – Hear –
c. 1863

The first stanza of "The Spirit is the Conscious Ear" speaks of the galvanizing event of her life, Edward Dickinson's seduction. Then, after the over-arching question of how she could abide this atrocity for a lifetime is how this incestuous relationship went undetected for more than one hundred fifty years, even as yearly the poet's readership grows and as the mountainous scholastic literature continues to rise. Perhaps part of the answer is that the poet grew increasingly iconic, and we the readers placed ourselves at a greater distance, "Outside the Castle –", not to mention from the beginning the machinations of a number of editors, the plurality of publishers, and those numerous parties and entities of copyright holders that inevitably grew institutionally with the concomitant investment issues, both emotional and financial.

Catharine MacKinnon, in her chapter "Equality and Speech" from *Only Words*, provides an immaculate overlay fitting this belief:

> These days, censorship occurs less through explicit state policy than
> through official and unofficial privileging of powerful groups and

---

§   The year of the earliest extant manuscript apparently could not be ascertained nor conjectured by Johnson; see xi. All unknown dates (per Johnson) will be indicated in this manner.

viewpoints. This is accomplished through silencing in many forms and enforced by the refusal of publishers and editors to publish, or publish well, uncompromised expressions of dissent that make them uncomfortable by challenging the distribution of power, including sexual power.[147]

(Those through simple devotion to Emily Dickinson are also complicit by insisting she be chaste in her preoccupation with poetry.)

Yet making it all the more intriguing is that the two-fold central question of the poet's life—who was her so-called "mystery lover" and why did she become a recluse—has never gone unasked by each new generation of reader and scholar and always with the presumption that these two presupposed facts of her life were somehow connected. A highly perforated connection, as he was a "father-god", and ultimately her phases of reclusion was an act of autonomy, not a broken heart—the connection true only insofar as shame severely circumscribed the base of her life—inscribing it with a constant duplicity.

XXII

Living beneath the timber of secrecy, Emily Dickinson in her poem below speaks to friend Kate Scott Anthon. Her heartrending accounting came later in her life and poetry, and here the nature of this secret is most palpable as it conveys the poet nearly engulfed by the scope of Edward Dickinson's betrayal.

1410
I shall not murmur if at last
The ones I loved below
Permission have to understand
For what I shunned them so –
Divulging it would rest my Heart
But it would ravage theirs –
Why, Katie, Treason has a Voice –
But mine – dispels – in Tears.
c. 1877

The gist of this poem is in the first two lines of [1167]"Alone and in a Circumstance" which continues long, ingeniously detailing her dissociation, as one deprived of a life and without any possibility of retribution.[1409]"Could mortal lip divine" also describes the breaking down of emotion-ladened speech. Next, "The Murmur of a Bee" tells of maintaining her secret and gives a justification and rationale, each stanza more covert, and is unique among her poems, based on a presupposition of self-questioning, and her wonderment. The poet in turn assumes she is responsible for what happened, a characteristic assumption of mistaken responsibility by children, continued into adulthood, who were abused physically, and emotionally.

The first stanza's lines, "'Twere easier to die – / Than tell – ", bring into focus the meaning of the poem, particularly the extreme "easier to die" statement; but the poet first softly speculates that it could have been the enchanting hum of a bee causing her to succumb to what she could not say, then a passion perhaps induced by her coming menses, and a warning not to judge, then last, the moment at dawn when he came to her—a refrain in her poetry.

155
The Murmur of a Bee
A Witchcraft – yieldeth me –
If any ask me why –
'Twere easier to die –
Than tell –

The Red upon the Hill
Taketh away my will-
If anybody sneer –
Take care – for God is here –
That's all.

The Breaking of the Day
Addeth to my Degree –
If any ask me how –
Artist – who drew me so –
Must tell!
c. 1860

Her keen sense of play and love of drama ([595]"Like Mighty Foot Lights – burned the Red"), of its seriousness ([741]"Drama's Vitallest Expression is the Common Day") were lively capacities, possessing a resourcefulness and overall acuteness, which Edward Dickinson exploited—for the show and charade—of a prolonged elaborate concealment. Her own preoccupation, obsession, with this she makes known in [1331]"Wonder – is not precisely Knowing".

She learned early on the bonds of treachery and the need to navigate powerful household cross-currents, the imperative of protecting egos, cues to be alert for, and with deception on a grand scale, the quicksilver art of dissimulation ([1327]"The Symptom of the Gale – "). [1771]"How fleet – how indiscreet an one – ", a four-line poem, cautions of the willful, impulsive behavior of errant love.

778

This that would greet – an hour ago –
Is quaintest Distance – now –
Had it a Guest from Paradise –
Nor glow, would it, nor bow –

Had it a notice from the Noon
Nor beam would it nor warm –
Match me the Silver Reticence –
Match me the Solid Calm –
c. 1863

The big tent or circus motif of the poem below turns nearly line-by-line with snake-like insinuation of illicit meetings. A Big Top of the outdoors is found once more on a diminutive scale in [1097]"Dew – is the Freshet in the Grass – ", with two poems making reference to a child's entrance into the woods on a mid-week afternoon. (Wednesday she specified for the second time in all of her poems, and provocatively, a God that might nap, oblivious of them, in [413]"I never felt at Home – Below – ".)

243

I've known a Heaven, like a Tent –
To wrap its shining Yards –
Pluck up its stakes, and disappear –
Without the sound of Boards
Or Rip of Nail – Or Carpenter –
But just the miles of Stare –
That Signalize a Show's Retreat –
In North America –

No Trace – no Figment of the Thing
That dazzled, Yesterday,
No Ring – no Marvel –
Men, and Feats –
Dissolved as utterly –
As Bird's far Navigation
Discloses just a Hue –
A plash of Oars, a Gaiety –
Then swallowed up, of View.
c. 1861

By her own account, the last time, an afternoon, she was to be alone with her father before his death, long past the time of any sexual liaison ([1164]"Were it to be the last"), was still with this ingrained, habitual subterfuge, however slight, when she "invented an absence for Mother."[148]

XXIII

Writing enabled the poet to momentarily elude the control of her tyrannical father and curatively deal with its ravages. The truth about her life was relegated to her poetry, divulged upon the openness of a page, but unpublished; the poet's creative life was doomed to universal invisibility—poems in drawers or in letters to friends, which Emily Dickinson privately emended, as she edited and bound her poetry in fascicles.[149] She also sent through the hedge of the Evergreens two hundred seventy-six poems to her sister-in-law Susan Dickinson and "almost three times as many" to Colonel Higginson.[150] The three following poems are samples of the range of preoccupation that percolated with the nature and the keeping of secrets. In the first, her secret is safe with the omniscient; in the second, it is buried deep in her soul; in the last, she concludes it preferable to live all alone with a secret.

835
Nature and God – I neither knew
Yet Both so well knew me
They startled, like Executors
Of My identity.

Yet Neither told – that I could learn –
My Secret as secure
As Herschel's private interest
Or Mercury's affair –
c. 1864

1385
"Secrets" is a daily word
Yet does not exist –
Muffled – it remits surmise –
Murmured – it has ceased –
Dungeoned in the Human Breast
Doubtless secrets lie –
But that Grate inviolate –
Goes nor comes away

———

Nothing with a Tongue or Ear –
Secrets stapled there
Will emerge but once – and dumb –
To the Sepulchre –
c. 1879

381
A Secret told –
Ceases to be a Secret – then –
A Secret – kept –
That – can appal but One –

Better of it – continual be afraid –
Than it –
And Whom you told it to – beside –
c. 1862

Then as a woman, having to hide herself as lover—the sanctuary of air—denied the delicious narcissism of lovers. In [703]"Out of sight? What of that?" there is an admission of risk and a denial that asks "what of it?" The poet equates their invisibility as lovers with that of the skies—which they yet need to hide under—in [1060]"Air has no Residence, no Neighbor,". "The pungent atom in the Air" is a saucy contradiction of the aroma left of semen.

1191
The pungent atom in the Air
Admits of no debate –
All that is named of Summer Days
Relinquished our Estate –

For what Department of Delight
As positive are we
As Limit of Dominion
Or Dams – of Ecstasy –
c. 1871

191
The Skies can't keep their secret!
They tell it to the Hills –
The Hills just tell the Orchards –
And they – the Daffodils!

A Bird – by chance – that goes that way –
Soft overhears the whole –
If I should bribe the little Bird –
Who knows but *she* would tell?

I think I won't – however –
It's finer – not to know –
If Summer were *an Axiom* –
What sorcery had *Snow?*

So keep your secret – Father!
I would not – if I could,
Know what the Sapphire Fellows, do,
In your new-fashioned world!
c. 1860

[1338]"What tenements of clover" or a tantalizing [691]"Would you like summer? Taste of ours.", give particularities, the different occupations, of summer life outdoors, with the latter mainly itemizing the enchanting benefits of the summer offerings. The first among them is an exhortation to purchase pleasure as one would at a bazaar. The blue sky as harbor is reiterated in "What tenements of clover", where not a rhythm, movement—trace of a tryst—is to be threatened by any wonder, let alone suspicion. [1339]"A Bee his burnished Carriage" reads autobiographically, especially herself as a rose and humble recipient of pleasure. The mysterious [627]"The Tint I cannot take – is best –" that to begin with seems to be something about indigo (a deep violet-blue) eye shadow and Cleopatra, but veers in the fourth and fifth stanzas to the subject of a secret beheld by the countryside. [345]"Funny – to be a Century – " and [346]"Not probable – The barest Chance – " share as well the elements of secrecy and the outdoors of birds and a demure earth.

The following poem shows a small figure discernible only by color, in gambol or repose to be seen distantly in the Pelham hills, a place of assignation in the Dickinson's neighborhood.[151] In this poem are examples of her supremely capable Shakespearean, word play. The poet is the "Lady" and is both "A Lady red – " and "A Lady white – ", who goes as a "Lily" in the field. The "red" and "white" are self-referential—again her auburn hair and white skin. "'Resurrection'" is a blasphemous sexual euphemism.

74
A Lady red – amid the Hill
Her annual secret keeps!

———

A Lady white, within the Field
In placid Lily sleeps!

The tidy Breezes, with their Brooms
Sweep vale – and hill – and tree!
Prithee, My pretty Housewives!
Who may expected be?

The Neighbors do not yet suspect!
The Woods exchange a smile!
Orchard, and Buttercup, and Bird-
In such a little while!

And yet, how still the Landscape stands!
How nonchalant the Hedge!
As if the "Resurrection"
Were nothing very strange!
c. 1859

In contrast to the happy audacity found in these poems, a late one states an aloneness that could not be abolished: [1603]"The going from a world we know", also later, she wrote of our mortality in [1634]"Talk not to me of Summer Trees".

Parenthetically, an intriguing utilization of the color pink is observed daubed here and there in the landscape of her poems. [6]"Frequently the woods are pink – " then in [22]"All these my banners be." a last line refers to swamps in June of that color, and in [136]"Have you got a Brook in your little heart," there is a description of birds that blush. A shawl in [1412]"Shame is the shawl of Pink". The poet describes the pinked projects [1748]"The reticent volcano keeps" and then a pink military simile in [1529]"'Tis Seasons since the Dimpled War". Her sensuous use of the color is found in the randy, [1641]"Betrothed to Righteousness might be" as well as in [1332]"Pink – small – and punctual – ", but an evanescent innocence in [1394]"Whose Pink career may have a close", and sweetness in [1578]"Blossoms will run away," then imparts whimsy in [1520]"The stem of a departed Flower" and creates [1670]"In Winter in my Room" a magical worm.

XXIV

[322]"There came a Day at Summer's full," is an amazing poem beginning with a summer day, moving to its close returning home, then beyond to an afterlife, as the poet and her father ascend to a new matrimonial union melded of love and pain. I think it is in these certain, and few, instances of poem making that Emily Dickinson was most reaching, successfully, in an endeavor to rectify her sexual

response to her father. Here, the poet first states the bliss of a summer day and, all for her, of blessed perfection. She then metaphorically describes the physicality of lovemaking, a sacrament of transubstantiation, wordless as His Body unclothed, a Holy Communion of ecstatic exchange. (The last stanza of "My Worthiness is all my Doubt – " also recalls the church image, "So I the undivine abode / Of His Elect Content – / Conform my Soul – as 'twere a Church, / Unto Her Sacrament – ".)

There is a bond of shared agony and a belief that in the afterlife, human passions of joy and suffering merit marriage. This facet of belief, a place somewhere in the beyond for their being together, always, is again voiced in [1643]"Extol thee – could I? Then I will".

A long ways removed and generalized in his pragmatic spirit was Samuel Fowler's belief that everyone buried remain in pairs, which she enumerates in [984]"'Tis Anguish grander than Delight." A Congregationalist belief was that if both husband and wife were "saved" in Christ, then both would be reunited in Heaven, and if not, then one would have to languish for an eternity without the other. His particular belief was of the commingling of dust of husband and wife which he upheld as a civic priority by stating as Chairman in a Report of the Committee on the Burying Ground, that "There is a feeling in our natures, which exists strongly . . . that as they were united among the living" that this dust be marital dust "in the congregation of the dead."[152] It was only after Lucretia's death in 1840 that his body was disinterred in Ohio and buried next to her, a stone's throw from the northern grounds of his Old Homestead.[153]

The poet's own sense of what actually occurs is found in her down-to-earth poem [1330]"Without a smile – Without a Throe".

Secret to the grave, but not beyond, Emily Dickinson intimates having a confidant in posterity, distant, reversed in time, evoking monuments of pharaohs—and unabashed, states that we shall see.

664
Of all the Souls that stand create –
I have elected – One –
When Sense from Spirit – files away –
And Subterfuge – is done –
When that which is – and that which was –
Apart – intrinsic – stand –
And this brief Drama in the flesh –
Is shifted – like a Sand –
When Figures show their royal Front –
And Mists – are carved away,
Behold the Atom – I preferred –
To all the lists of Clay!
c. 1862

———

His Seduction

XXV

"Shame need not crouch
In such a world as ours;
Shame, stand erect
The universe is yours!"

643
I could suffice for Him, I knew –
He – could suffice for Me –
Yet Hesitating Fractions – Both
Surveyed Infinity –

"Would I be Whole" He sudden broached –
My syllable rebelled –
'Twas face to face with Nature – forced –
'Twas face to face with God –

Withdrew the Sun – to Other Wests –
Withdrew the furthest Star
Before Decision – stooped to speech –
And then – be audibler

The Answer of the Sea unto
The Motion of the Moon –
Herself adjust Her Tides – unto –
Could I – do else – with Mine?
c. 1862

"I could suffice for Him, I knew – " is a poem of the seduction of Emily Dickinson, as impulse and destiny arc in her body. "'Would I be Whole" He sudden broached – / My syllable rebelled – / 'Twas face to face with nature – forced – / 'Twas face to face with God – ", the spectacle of her private universe changing forever: "Withdrew the Sun – to Other Wests – / Withdrew the furthest Star / Before Decision – stooped to speech – / And then – be audibler". Again later with, [615]"Our journey had advanced – ", there is an awestruck recounting, retrospective.

190
He was weak, and I was strong – then –
So He let me lead him in –
I was weak, and He was strong then –
So I let him lead me – Home.

'Twasn't far – the door was near –
'Twasn't dark – for He went – too –
'Twasn't loud, for He said nought –
That was all I cared to know.

Day knocked – and we must part –
Neither – was strongest – now –
He strove – and I strove – too
We didn't do it – tho'!
c. 1860

506
He touched me, so I live to know
That such a day, permitted so,
I groped upon his breast –
It was a boundless place to me
And silenced, as the awful sea
Puts minor streams to rest.

And now, I'm different from before,
As if I breathed superior air –
Or brushed a Royal Gown –
My feet, too, that had wandered so –
My Gypsy face – transfigured now –
To tenderer Reknown –

Into this Port, if I might come,
Rebecca, to Jerusalem,
Would not so ravished turn –
Nor Persian, baffled at her shrine
Lift such a Crucifixal sign
To her imperial Sun.
c. 1862

1721
He was my host – he was my guest,
I never to this day
If I invited him could tell,
Or he invited me.

So infinite our intercourse
So intimate, indeed,
Analysis as capsule seemed
To keeper of the seed.
c.?

   Emily Dickinson, captive and convinced from childhood of her father's love, never had a real defense against his array of manipulative powers and, once sexually aroused, was betrayed by her body, creating permanent apprehension.

1090
I am afraid to own a Body –
I am afraid to own a Soul –
Profound – precarious Property –
Possession, not optional –

Double Estate – entailed at pleasure
Upon an unsuspecting Heir –
Duke in a moment of Deathlessness
And God, for a Frontier.
c. 1866

(In the haunting [351]"I felt my life with both my hands" we find a protracted crisis of being, and then is proffered a pre-cursing Freudian, hypothetical understanding in [1054]"Not to discover weakness is".)

If there could have been a single axis of her being, it was the poet's standing relative to her father and his focus, enduring a fate that rose and fell in his eyes.

751
My Worthiness is all my Doubt –
His Merit – all my fear –
Contrasting which, my quality
Do lowlier – appear –

Lest I should insufficient prove
For His beloved Need –
The Chiefest Apprehension
Upon my thronging Mind –

'Tis true – that Deity to stoop
Inherently incline –
For nothing higher than Itself
Itself can rest upon –

So I – the undivine abode
Of His Elect Content –
Conform my Soul – as 'twere a Church,
Unto Her Sacrament –
c. 1863

738
You said that I "was Great" – one Day –
Then "Great" it be – if that please Thee –
Or Small – or any size at all –
Nay – I'm the size suit Thee –

Tall – like the Stag – would that?
Or lower – like the Wren –
Or other heights of Other Ones
I've seen?

Tell which – it's dull to guess –
And I must be Rhinoceros
Or Mouse
At once – for Thee –

So say – if Queen it be –
Or Page – please Thee –
I'm that – or nought –
Or other thing – if other thing there be –
With just this Stipulus –
I suit Thee –
c. 1863

In the poet's lifelong performance of family roles, of a dutiful daughter, loving sister, and aunt, there would be the mere way stations for Edward Dickinson, his seeming love a conditional, vagrant regard to assure his own gratification. Not so for the poet; it was [1314]"When a Lover is a Beggar" even posthumously, eternally. [1383]"Long Years apart – can make no" splits no difference, in body or spirit—whether a moment or a millennia, when at her most enamored or idealistic.

Nonetheless, after her father's death, and by then almost forty-four years old, the poet wrote in the guise of simple and brief adult ruminations—first, that God entrusted our behavior to us, so the worst rebounds to Him ([1461]"'Heavenly Father' – take to thee"), which is restated in [1403]"My Maker – let me be", then second, that we do not know when we are to be born or when we will die ([1462]"We knew not that we were to live – ")—each illustrating very real thinking about her father's behavior. In both there are striking insinuations in word choices: ""Heavenly Father" – take to thee" uses the image of an uninhibited hand; in "We knew not that we were to live– " is an article of clothing, perhaps a nightgown; then the last two lines declare an intrusion and, by inference, of a God-like figure. (Also [1205]"Immortal is an ample word" uses the image of a roving, upper hand.)

THE RAPE

XXVI

The bandage was white, as was the dress worn daily after her father's death by the reclusive poet, a small, finely stitched garment that hung in Emily Dickinson's closet for years on public display for visitors to her upstairs bedroom in the Old Homestead.

512
The Soul has Bandaged moments –
When too appalled to stir –
She feels some ghastly Fright come up
And stop to look at her –

Salute her – with long fingers –
Caress her freezing hair –
Sip, Goblin, from the very lips
The Lover – hovered – o'er –
Unworthy, that a thought so mean
Accost a Theme – so – fair –

The soul has moments of Escape –
When bursting all the doors –
She dances like a Bomb, abroad,
And swings upon the Hours,

As do the Bee – delirious borne –
Long Dungeoned from his Rose –
Touch Liberty – then know no more,
But Noon, and Paradise –

The Soul's retaken moments –
When, Felon led along,
With shackles on the plumed feet,
And staples, in the Song,

The Horror welcomes her, again,
These, are not brayed of Tongue –
c. 1862

This is a narrative of dissociation as the poet, personifying the soul, describes her life as Emily through two major inferences: "Bandaged moments – " and their opposite, "moments of Escape – ", both expressive of polar, intercurrent experiences of catatonia, or limitless overflowing, reiterated in the lines "When too appalled to stir – " or "When bursting all the doors – ". "The Soul has Bandaged moments – " has set in its midst a line denoting an ecstatic element in her life and poetry: "As do the Bee – delirious borne – " full and free, but in the lines above, the soul informs, "Sip, Goblin, from the very lips / The Lover hovered o'er". In this way the poet tells of a double life, the dichotomy, or split, she struggled almost lifelong to keep bound, a life with "the Goblin Bee – / That will not state – its sting.". (About the goblin there is another and resonant use of the word "sting" in the last line of [156]"You love me – you are sure – ").

Emily Dickinson needed to live as though her life had a strictly conventional bent, fruited with few options, a hard Calvinist fruit. But living in the false domain of this relationship, she felt defrauded, expressed in the poem [476]"I meant to have but modest needs – "; or she is wishful for warm and frank days ([646]"I think to Live – may be a Bliss").

"No Goblin – on the Bloom – " is desirous of a vertical, unaffrighted reality, but as mandated by Edward Dickinson, instead the poet was futilely striving behind a facade in the unpredictable, weighty, and shadowy life of when "The Horror welcomes her, again," the soul in bandages. Then again resounding pitiably in the magisterial, [410]"The first Day's Night had come – ".

A "Big my Secret but it's bandaged – " also appears in the poem [1737]"Rearrange a "Wife's" affection!" The "bandaged" moments in these two poems, and there are only three in her poetry, were to conceal as much as to heal. The third poem, [1323]"I never hear that one is dead" conveys that even if one were prompted to say what she believed, she could not because of the bandage.

Another poem with a customary rarity of precision concerning solely her state of mind is [937]"I felt a Cleaving in my Mind – ". And there is a compartmentalization, described differently, matter-of-factly, in the third stanza of [777]"The Loneliness One dare not sound – ", having in its entirety a wide cavernous meaning. It is again shown with brevity in the poem [837]"How well I knew Her not".

[708]"I sometimes drop it, for a Quick – " is a ruminative version of the relatively fewer poems concerned with pain in extremis—the stalk of her being twained.

A poem of an almost jaunty tenor, [364]"The Morning after Woe – " describes what it is like to be feeling sharply separate from a world of blossoms and birds, beyond the particular imagery, the poem gives an inner sense, and sensation of this.

In [510]"It was not Death, for I stood up," the poet brings the outside world into the poem with the peal of noonday bells. There is an end brought to the agitation, even animation, in [918]"Only a Shrine, but Mine – " as supplicant, obvious in her need.

XXVII

Contemplating the import of pain, (over the years recollected, of horrors, details, isolated images, obscured in a froth of memory, yet evoking indelibly, persecution and intractable pain); and reviewing "The Soul has Bandaged moments – ", "'Twas like a Maelstrom, with a notch," I saw the fulcrum, the contours of her soul, of conscience, conflict, and self-condemnation, the twist more of agony than comes with a broken heart, even a complex one.

414
'Twas like a Maelstrom, with a notch,
That nearer, every Day,
Kept narrowing its boiling Wheel
Until the Agony

Toyed coolly with the final inch
Of your delirious Hem –
And you dropt, lost,
When something broke –
And let you from a Dream –

As if a Goblin with a Gauge –
Kept measuring the Hours –
Until you felt your Second
Weigh, helpless, in his Paws –

And not a Sinew – stirred – could help,
And sense was setting numb –
When God – remembered – and the Fiend
Let go, then, Overcome –

———

As if your Sentence stood – pronounced –
And you were frozen led
From Dungeon's luxury of Doubt
To Gibbets, and the Dead –

And when the Film had stitched your eyes
A Creature gasped "Reprieve"!
Which Anguish was the utterest – then –
To perish, or to live?
c. 1862

The extraordinary brilliance of Emily Dickinson's self-awareness and coherence in this poem reveals in neurological detail the deep turmoil of a soul: "Until you felt your second / Weigh, . . . / . . . / And sense was setting numb". Then she describes the penumbra of psychotic pain: "And when the Film had stitched your eyes". On the whole, it is a poem of tribulation—in the eternal moment—as the poet equates the pain of living with the pain of extinction.

What is deeply moving is that as Emily Dickinson presents in these major poems an adult pain, she relives the painful effects of childhood trauma, not outlived, connecting us to her childhood experience of powerlessness and persecution in [612]"Upon me – like a Claw – / I could no more remove" and [874]"They'll recollect how cold I looked . . . / Who cannot thank Them for the Ice". As in "The Soul has Bandaged moments – ", she describes being "too appalled to stir" and the soul's "freezing hair"; and once more in "'Twas like a Maelstrom, with a notch," she says "And not a Sinew – stirred – could help," "And you were frozen led". Which again the poet re-experienced in the monumental summing up in a poem written of her adulthood, [341]"After great pain, a formal feeling comes – ": a cold already long familiar.

599
There is a pain – so utter –
It swallows substance up –
Then covers the Abyss with Trance –
So Memory can step
Around – across – upon it –
As one within a swoon –
Goes safely –where an open eye –
Would drop Him – Bone by Bone.
c. 1862

The eight lines of this poem are an abbreviation of "'Twas like a Maelstrom, with a notch,". Whether perseveration or a variation, the lines "There is a pain – so utter – " and "Until the Agony / Toyed coolly with the final inch" are altered echoes of one another, the latter from "'Twas like a Maelstrom, with a notch,". (Within an ecstatic context, she also reuses images: "The Depths upon my soul was notched – / As Floods on – Whites of Wheels – ".)

The poems, ruminations of ruin, of a more removed quality, are heard in [581]"I found the words to every thought" and [748]"Autumn – overlooked my Knitting – ", each employ the word "cochineal," a crimson dye of virgin insects, the cochineal having a brilliant bodily fluid extracted by crushing and drying.

As a desire, suicide, or self-extinction, seldom occurs in an Emily Dickinson poem even abstracted in her images or metaphors—despite the nearly continual and painful tumult of this poet's life—with the exception of these four: [351]"I felt my life with both my hands", [50]"I haven't told my garden yet – ", and the even more oblique [908]"'Tis Sunrise – Little Maid – Hast Thou" and the angry threat of [277]"What if I say I shall not wait!".

The Bride

XXVIII

B efore being a poet, becoming an "Immortal," Emily Dickinson was a young woman of her time residing on Main Street in Amherst, Massachusetts, squarely in the mid-nineteenth century, and whose main hope of leaving her family, finding release, was to be married, a contractual and circumscribed shift in social standing, going from her father's house to her husband's, as her own mother had done, ([586]"We talked as Girls do −"). For Emily Dickinson, however, it was only through the creation of the poem that this status, its promise, could be objectified at all, and in the idealized way that she conceived of marriage, conferring a christening quality. The poet was sorely and permanently denied the sanctity of matrimonial bliss—fornication meant forfeiture—of this longed for connubial state. Her poem "All that I do" establishes the frank sexual tension in the household:

1496
All that I do
Is in review
To his enamored mind
I know his eye
Where e'er I ply
Is pushing close behind
Not any Port
Nor any flight
But he doth there preside
What omnipresence lies in wait
For her to be a Bride
c. 1880

XXIX

A poem inspired the week of Valentine's, the first in *The Complete Poems*, begins "Oh the Earth was *made* for lovers, for damsel, and hopeless swain," and by the fifth line has made a union of the two, so the bride can assuredly be viewed as the earliest of the poet's figures, most archetypal of Emily Dickinson's preoccupations, producing a significant and lasting image in her poetry.

A late-life poem, and if the dating is accurate written two years before her death, begins [1620]"Circumference thou Bride of Awe"; then a posthumous marriage was envisioned in an 1862 poem, [625]"'Twas a long Parting – but the time".

Because of the importance and centrality of these poems, monumental in motif and meaning, an index is included at the end of this section so it can be readily viewed that all the poems about the Bride from *The Complete Poems* have been brought together for scrutiny regarding this interpretation.

The "Bride" poems in the order given here form a soliloquy, beginning victorious and jubilant with "Title divine – is mine!" Then in "Her sweet Weight on my Heart a Night", she grasps that she is dreaming, and deceived.

"A solemn thing – it was – I said – " continues to ponder the soulful seriousness of being a bride, and she can only imagine marital bliss in "The World – stands – solemner – to me – ", deciding to tell herself she is wed, her inner world altering to meet the generosity, grace, bestowed by this rarified state. "I am ashamed – I hide – " concedes she is "So late a Dowerless Girl" who dresses futility in fantasy—alone, how could she know the jewels to choose?—donning clothes of pompadour, reshaping hairdo round to oval, have royal comportment, without pride or shame. At last, declares "Baptized – this Day – A Bride – ", which reveals Emily Dickinson's recurrent idea of baptism as a marital rite. The poet seems to be saying she was given over to her father at baptism, secreting in the last line her secret. The series comes to a scintillating close with a breezy, multi-faceted, and wiser "Morning – means "Milking" – to the Farmers".

1072
Title divine – is mine!
The Wife – without the Sign!
Acute Degree – conferred on me –
Empress of Calvary!
Royal – all but the Crown!
Betrothed – without the swoon
God sends us Women –

When you – hold – Garnet to Garnet –
Gold – to Gold –
Born – Bridalled – Shrouded –
In a Day –
Tri Victory
"My Husband" – women say –
Stroking the Melody –
Is *this* – the way?
c. 1862

"Title divine – is mine!' could not be more clear in all its meanings and hopeful credulity—finding worth, identity in another—the poet's delight in the scheme of a "Tri Victory" of being born a woman.

518
Her sweet Weight on my Heart a Night
Had scarcely deigned to lie –
When, stirring, for Belief's delight,
My Bride had slipped away –

If 'twas a Dream – made solid – just
The Heaven to confirm –
Or if Myself were dreamed of Her –
The power to presume –

With Him remain – who unto Me –
Gave – even as to All –
A Fiction superseding Faith –
By so much – as 'twas real –
c. 1862

The above poem is a triple reverie, first, a dream of self as bride. The dreamer—the spiritual "she" as bride, this "Belief's Delight"—wakes, and "My Bride had slipped away – ". Then, "If 'twas a Dream – made solid – just / The Heaven to confirm – " asserts that "If" the dream is "made solid" or real, all that is left is for it to be blessed. Last, "The power to presume – " is to step into the shoes of the bride's dream of her, returning to the progenitor, poem maker.

Then as if to account for this convoluted construct, the mutability of the real and unreal, a transparency and interchangeability of bride, dreamer, and poet, Emily Dickinson lays it at her father's feet: "With Him remain – who unto Me – / Gave – even as to All – ", admitting that she, foremostly, was not "exempt from his pathology"[154] and seeing that anybody entering his sphere was subject to the nefarious modus operandi of Edward Dickinson: "A Fiction superseding Faith – / By so much – as 'twas real – ", the complete deception of a virtual reality. The identical idea is repeated in "I think to Live – may be a Bliss", the delusion and self-deception he freely imparted to others.

271
A solemn thing – it was – I said –
A woman – white – to be –
And wear – if God should count me fit –
Her blameless mystery –

A hallowed thing – to drop a life
Into the purple well –
Too plummetless – that it return –
Eternity – until –

I pondered how the bliss would look –
And would it feel as big –
When I could take it in my hand –
As hovering – seen – through fog –

And then – the size of this "small" life –
The Sages – call it small –
Swelled – like Horizons – in my vest –
And I sneered – softly – "small"!
c. 1861

In the sanctity of marriage, lips of devotion and purity partake of eternity, "the purple well – ". However, posed against the physical realm, "When I could take it in my hand – / As hovering – seen – through fog – ", the poet probes and then asks whether this idealized "bliss" would feel as "big" if she really possessed it. Inversely, her human life, though "small," "Swelled like Horizons – in my vest – " (her breasts she disparages as also "'small'!").

493

The World – stands – solemner – to me –
Since I was wed – to Him –
A modesty befits the soul
That bears another's – name –
A doubt – if it be fair – indeed –
To wear that perfect – pearl –
The Man – upon the Woman – binds –
To clasp her soul – for all –
A prayer, that it more angel – prove –
A whiter Gift – within –
To that munificence, that chose –
So unadorned – a Queen –
A Gratitude – that such be true –
It had esteemed the Dream –
Too beautiful – for Shape to prove –
Or posture – to redeem!
c. 1862

In this poem she again speaks of the holiness of marriage, and actualized, from a newfound perspective "That bears another's – name – ", hoping for greater perfection, "A whiter Gift" to meet this "munificence"– more than she can live up to – "It had esteemed the Dream / Too beautiful – for Shape to prove", "a Queen" without a pearl. Beauty that cannot be shown, measurably defined, or completely grasped, so beautiful it is—"Or posture – to redeem!"—upheld, straight enough, for approbation on high.

473

I am ashamed – I hide –
What right have I – to be a Bride –
So late a Dowerless Girl –
Nowhere to hide my dazzled Face –
No one to teach me that new Grace –
Nor introduce – my Soul –

Me to adorn – How – tell –
Trinket – to make Me beautiful –
Fabrics of Cashmere –
Never a Gown of Dun – more –
Raiment instead – of Pompadour –
For Me – My soul – to wear –

Fingers – to frame my Round Hair
Oval – as Feudal Ladies wore –
Far Fashions – Fair –
Skill – to hold my Brow like an Earl –
Plead – like a Whippoorwill –
Prove – like a Pearl –
Then, for Character –
Fashion My Spirit quaint – white –
Quick – like a Liquor –
Gay – like Light –
Bring Me my best Pride –
No more ashamed –
No more to hide –
Meek – let it be – too proud – for Pride –
Baptized – this Day – A Bride –
c. 1862

   Now despite declaring in several ways to have lost her chance at marriage (prospects of which a tender articulation is found in "We talked as Girls do" – "), I am ashamed – I hide – ", "So late a Dowerless Girl – ", and motherless, never "Fingers – to frame my Round Hair / Oval as Feudal Ladies wore – ", she yet does describe herself as a bride, radiant and transformed, feeling awkward and not any longer knowing herself except by donning finery "Never a Gown of Dun – more – ". "Then, for Character – " she gives herself a new spiritual identity, "quaint," pure and effervescent, "Baptized – this Day – a Bride", born to be her father's bride and "too proud – for Pride – ".

300
"Morning" – means "Milking" – to the Farmer –
Dawn – to the Teneriffe –
Dice – to the Maid –
Morning means just Risk – to the Lover –
Just revelation – to the Beloved –

Epicures – date a Breakfast – by it –
Brides – an Apocalypse –
Worlds – a Flood –
Faint-going Lives – Their Lapse from Sighing –
Faith – The Experiment of Our Lord –
c. 1862

This poem is her variation, riff, on facing the day, the predictable, mild prospect of milking, oppositely, gambling, and a sense of risk fortified by catastrophic notions. (The poet recollects Shelley's "Teneriffe," the fabulous tree from where spiritual whispers were heard above—"which makes night day"; in mundane terms, she has her days and nights turned around.) In the first stanza, the poet traces the configurations and course of the relationship with her father, "Risk" in aspirations of the "Lover," and in the second stanza, "revelation" anticipation of the "Beloved," and moves on to epicurean fulfillment, "Breakfast." Then "Brides" awaken to a new day as an "Apocalypse" and revelation whipped up to prophesy, global in dimension, "Flood," not for the faint-hearted, with the poet finally declaring "Faith – The Experiment of Our Lord – ".

She categorically assigned meanings to morning in the poem "Morning" – means "Milking" . . . , with it certainly meaning risk to the lover and all revealing to the beloved, a realm of ideas she seems to be further expanding and particularizing in the following poems: [480]"Why do I love" You, Sir?", because he is the sunrise, she can see; [638]"To my small Hearth His fire came – " and was quickly lit; [1739]"Some say goodnight – at night – " but she does so at day; [1095]"To Whom the Mornings stand for Nights," what must the middle of the night be! [1186]"Too few the mornings be," for which there was hardly a place, peculiarly elusive, as she had no say in designing their time together. (Possibly, this depiction in her poems of the disruptive timing of her father's demands was to gain an orientation, within a charged, and lonely circumstance.)

Among them there is also a celebratory aspect, exultant and commemorative. But most of all, nothing between her and her father was to go unnoted in this journal of poems, especially as she was left holding a double-handled cup for the last lone bitter quaff.

Index of "Bride" Poems

XXX

From the windows of Emily Dickinson's home, usually her bedroom, in her poems, the sun's rising and setting appear in ways often startling and disarming and by more than beauty alone justifies. This effect could have been produced optically, an expression of abnormally light-sensitive eyes, or on the other end of the spectrum, by the unlawful, lustful incursions of Edward Dickinson.

A chronology, logical emotionally, can be made sequential, as a downward spiral, in the following poems, beginning with the heavily italicized [232]"The *Sun—just touched* the Morning–" then[197]"Morning – is the place for Dew – ", which repeats the deterministic, "Duke" in the poem, [273]"He put the Belt around my life – ". Then polarized [415]"Sunset at Night – is natural – " seems to describe her life eclipsed, [425]"Good Morning – Midnight – " speaks to emotional abandonment, and the gruesome [762]"The Whole of it came not at once – " conveys a cynical suffering. Finally, [1610]"Morning that comes but once," states that there is a price to pay.

The terms "Bride," "wife," and "housewife" are not interchangeable in the poems. The bride is chosen and supreme; a wife, cherished, has a position of eminent status, religious, setting the moral tone and tenets for the household; while the housewife in her poetry is a practitioner of the household arts.

The two poems below exemplify the meaning and spirit of the wife. In the first, she declares a status of "wife" that designates her a "Woman" of power, a "Czar" in another, better, "safer" world certainly compared to how her childhood felt—perhaps a sense of having leverage, bearing a little negotiation. It "was pain" which she believes is past, unnecessary to mull over. This was to prove momentary, if not momentarily delusory, for even in her last poems late in life, she wrote, [1598]"Who is it seeks my Pillow Nights – ".

199

I'm "wife" – I've finished that –

That other state –

I'm Czar – I'm "Woman" now –

It's safer so –

How odd the Girl's life looks
Behind this soft Eclipse –
I think that Earth feels so
To folks in Heaven – now –

This being comfort – then
That other kind – was pain –
But why compare?
I'm "Wife"! Stop there!
c. 1860

961
Wert Thou but ill – that I might show thee
How long a Day I could endure
Though thine attention stop not on me
Nor the least signal, Me assure –

Wert Thou but Stranger in ungracious country –
And Mine – the Door
Thou paused at, for a passing bounty –
No More –

Accused – wert Thou – and Myself – Tribunal –
Convicted – Sentenced – Ermine – not to Me
Half the Condition, thy Reverse – to follow –
Just to partake – the infamy –

The Tenant of the Narrow Cottage, wert Thou –
Permit to be
The Housewife in thy low attendance
Contenteth Me –

No Service hast Thou, I would not achieve it –
To die – or live –
The first – Sweet, proved I, ere I saw thee –
For Life – be Love –
c. 1864

The first two stanzas of the second poem above are a full-throated affirmation
of love, thus selflessly in successive stanzas she assures him that if he were ill,

alone, or if anyone were found out, she would be at his side, and even as the lowly housewife. ("The Tenant of the Narrow Cottage" brings to mind the Old Homestead split in two, rented on the one side by Edward Dickinson.) The poem ends by stating that there is nothing he could ask that she wouldn't do; to die of love for him would mean she had lived. "Just to partake – the infamy – " echoes the line "Forever of His fate to taste – " in her poem [246]"Forever at His side to walk – ".

As life would have it, Edward Dickinson predeceased his daughter in 1874, and to judge by the chronology set in *The Complete Poems*, a late poem (written about 1873, a year true to the sense of finale in the poem), there is a very last use of the image of the bride in the ending lines of [1257]"Dominion lasts until obtained – ".

WAITING

XXXI

834
Before He comes we weigh the Time!
'Tis Heavy and 'tis Light.
When He depart, an Emptiness
Is the prevailing Freight.
c. 1864

The poems of "Waiting" are all of those of that particular topic in *The Complete Poems*, as a theme was struck in her life and poetry, with poems both mundane and charged, speaking of longing and patience. Emily Dickinson was perpetually ensconced, voiceless, between the will and whim of her father. [1155]"Distance – is not the Realm of Fox"—the real one—is the distance where he might be from her. In [247]"What would I give to see his face?", the poet creates an opalescent glimpse of an inner child enraptured by a father whose actions were ruinous to her. At the end of the poem, there is a switch of gender of the object of adoration (the subject of the poem), which is the poet's wish to create a disguise.

In the Dickinson household, father's coming home had an especial note and notice that rose to a level of panic, indicative of the degree to which Edward Dickinson controlled their home lives ([889]"Crisis is a Hair"). From *Face to Face*: "Girls, your father is coming!"

> No matter what the calamity, no matter how stark the domestic emergency, by the time he reached the side piazza the peace of heaven's own morn lay thick upon the atmosphere .... Emily would vanish into the front hall, their mother peer about to be sure nothing was amiss—no

---

61

cat in a forbidden chair, the morning paper folded and in its place—no omission to disturb her approaching husband, . . . [155]

Daughter Emily's waiting constituted a separate reality from her family's ([570]"I could die – to know – ", [781]"To wait an Hour – is long – "). Perhaps the observable father-daughter presence was having their heads together, seeming no more than his seeking attention on a household or business matter, but it was most likely about his initiating the designation, confirmation, of time and place to meet, specified in [999]"Superfluous were the Sun" and implied in [850]"I sing to use the Waiting".

In a bubble of waiting, the poet projects herself wryly into her father's being: [207]"Tho' I get home how late – how late – "; a temporal eternity of an interminable wait is expressed by [1449]"I thought the Train would never come – " and in the poem below.

635
I think the longest Hour of all
Is when the Cars have come –
And we are waiting for the Coach –
It seems as though the Time

Indignant – that the Joy was come –
Did block the Gilded Hands –
And would not let the Seconds by –
But slowest instant – ends –

The Pendulum begins to count –
Like little Scholars – loud –
The steps grow thicker – in the Hall –
The Heart begins to crowd –

Then I – my timid service done –
Tho' service 'twas, of Love –
Take up my little Violin –
And further North – remove.
c. 1862

There are poems that could have come to her as she waited with a tense desire—passion taking a back seat to an imperial passivity—opportunities to garner perspectives of the kinds and various qualities of the passage of time:

"Before He comes we weigh the Time!" divulges "'Tis Heavy" and 'tis Light.", and "When He depart, an Emptiness". And in "Fitter to see Him, I may be", we learn that there is "Time to anticipate His Gaze – ". In "You taught me Waiting with Myself – ", we hear "You taught me fortitude of Fate – ", as the poet addresses the crux of her concern—the cross in this relationship—confronting shame. A rueful scan from the ironic "An Altitude of death, that could / No bitterer debar / Than Life – had done – before it – " to a rarified expression of her vulnerability in "The Heaven you know – to understand / That you be not ashamed / Of Me – in Christ's bright Audience".

Although reconfigured, she is still fretful in [412]"I read my sentence – steadily – ", to be repeated in the cerebral [105]"To hang our head – ostensibly – ", and yet again in [662]"Embarrassment of one another", and despite all her fortitude, an excoriating [362]"It struck me – every Day – ". (After her father's death she wrote in 1877 the mellowed "Shame is the shawl of Pink".)

740
You taught me Waiting with Myself –
Appointment strictly kept –
You taught me fortitude of Fate –
This – also – I have learnt –

An Altitude of Death, that could
No bitterer debar
Than Life – had done – before it –
Yet – there is a Science more –

The Heaven you know – to understand
That you be not ashamed
Of Me – in Christ's bright Audience
Upon the further Hand –
c. 1863

Finally, a discourse on the aesthetics and effects of the passage of time on human appearance is to be heard in "Fitter to see Him, I may be", a gentle perambulation through notions of change in beauty over time, with their final effect: "To make Me fairest of the Earth", "I only must not grow so new" or "I only must not change so fair". The thought then aspires to "But gain – thro' loss – Through Grief – obtain – / The Beauty that reward Him best – " and concludes that beauty enriched in mourning is spiritual and sustained.

968

Fitter to see Him, I may be
For the long Hindrance – Grace – to Me –
With Summers, and with Winters, grow,
Some passing Year – A trait bestow

To make Me fairest of the Earth –
The Waiting – then – will seem so worth
I shall impute with half a pain
The blame that I was chosen – then –

Time to anticipate His Gaze –
It's first – Delight – and then – Surprise –
The turning o'er and o'er my face
For Evidence it be the Grace –

He left behind One Day – So less
He seek Conviction, That – be This –

I only must not grow so new
That He'll mistake – and ask for me
Of me – when first unto the Door
I go – to Elsewhere go no more –

I only must not change so fair
He'll sigh – "The Other – She – is Where?"
The Love, tho', will array me right
I shall be perfect – in His sight –

If He perceive the other Truth –
Upon an Excellenter Youth –

How sweet I shall not lack in Vain –
But gain – thro' loss – Through Grief – obtain –
The Beauty that reward Him best –
The Beauty of Demand – at Rest –
c. 1864

    It would almost seem that Emily Dickinson wrote in 1874 a postscript to the poems of her waiting with [1153]"Through what transports of Patience", as that was the year of her father's death.

In the House

XXXII

"On that dear Frame the Years had worn"

463
I live with Him – I see His face –
I go no more away
For Visitor – or Sundown –
Death's single privacy

The Only One – forestalling Mine –
And that – by Right that He
Presents a Claim invisible –
No wedlock – granted Me –

I live with Him – I hear His Voice –
I stand alive – Today –
To witness to the Certainty
Of Immortality –

Taught Me – by Time – the lower Way –
Conviction – Every day –
That Life like This – is stopless –
Be Judgement – what it may –
c. 1862

In my several readings of *The Complete Poems* it gradually became evident that this relationship of Edward Dickinson's toward his daughter, was circumstantially, often enacted right at home, [1218]"Let my first Knowing be of thee".

In ways her forebears never could have thought or believed the rooms of the Old Homestead housed an invisible, forbidden home life ([398]"I had not minded – Walls – " and [532]"I tried to think a lonelier Thing"), of which Emily Dickinson reveals a blueprint through the use of several physical features in a number of her poems: [190]"He was weak, and I was strong – then – ... So I let him lead me – Home ... 'Twasn't far – the door was near – " or [293]"I got so I could take his name – ... I got so I could walk / That Angle in the floor," as she wrote of her bedroom—which place is the "Home" I believe is meant in [1423]"The fairest Home I ever knew".

The quiet upon a rural morning is when the poet could have heard from her bed, [1160]"He is alive, this morning – ", or what she wrote in the Lyman letters:

> [Father] ... says that his life has been passed in a wilderness or an island ... of late he says on an island. And so it is, for in the morning I hear his voice and methinks it comes from afar & has a sea tone & there is a hum of hoarseness about [it] & a suggestion of remoteness as far as the isle of Juan Fernandez.[156]

A description matching this discernment can be read in [955]"The Hollows round His eager Eyes", but instead of tone of voice, it is the look of Edward Dickinson stranded in his own pain.

XXXIII

The upstairs, of her "northern room" where [405]"It might be lonelier", was her bedroom ([472]"Except the Heaven had come so near – " and [638]"To my small Hearth His fire came – ").

1661
Guest am I to have
Light my northern room
Why to cordiality so averse to come
Other friends adjourn
Other bonds decay
Why avoid so narrowly
My fidelity –
c. ?

(from 635)
Take up my little Violin –
And further North – remove.

———

66

The stairs and "the Hall" (center hall upstairs) are clearly recognizable, traversed during a relationship known but to themselves.

461
A Wife – at Daybreak I shall be –
Sunrise – Hast thou a Flag for me?
At Midnight, I am but a Maid
How short it takes to make a Bride –
Then – Midnight, I have passed from thee
Unto the East, and Victory –

Midnight – Good Night! I hear them call,
The Angels bustle in the Hall –
Softly my Future climbs the Stair,
I fumble at my Childhood's prayer
So soon to be a Child no more –
Eternity, I'm coming – Sir,
Savior – I've seen the face – before!
c. 1862

The ecstatic question in [1095]"To Whom the Mornings stand for Nights," is answered in the poem above, "A Wife – at Daybreak I shall be– ". The poet's light of day as waves of fabric is here a banner with which she asks the sunrise to herald a new light of day, one of a lifetime for her. In this change in the childhood relationship with her father (apparently taking place abruptly early on), the poet in the last three lines declares she is soon no longer to be a child, and with startling connotation, reveals an imminent and familiar face as perpetrator.

1672
Lightly stepped a yellow star
To its lofty place –
Loosed the Moon her silver hat
From her lustral Face –
All of Evening softly lit
As an Astral Hall –
Father, I observed to Heaven,
You are punctual.
c. ?

(from 635)
The steps grow thicker – in the Hall –

Later, yet childlike, gleeful, [179]"If I could bribe them by a Rose", disguising her father in the plural third person, she writes of this same hall, from where she would need to be driven. In the last stanza of [640]"I cannot live with You – ", his door ajar, are the furtive glimpses of her father.

The view from her window ([768]"When I hoped, I recollect"), is reversed, schizoid, in this device of passing outside, looking up at her own window:

1285
I know Suspense – it steps so terse
And turns so weak away –
Besides – Suspense is neighborly
When I am riding by –

Is always at the Window
Though lately I descry
And mention to my Horses
The need is not of me –
c. 1873

The following poems objectify the enclosed passage, rooms, of this relationship.

1760
Elysium is as far as to
The very nearest Room
If in that Room a Friend await
Felicity or Doom –

What fortitude the Soul contains,
That it can so endure
The accent of a coming Foot –
The opening of a Door –
c. 1882

1767
Sweet hours have perished here;
    This is a mighty room;
Within its precincts hopes have played, –
    Now shadows in the tomb.
c. ?

To rendezvous at home, they were confined to where they could have only momentarily, and riskily, been occupied ([1434]"Go not too near a House of Rose –" and [1175]"We like a Hairsbreadth 'scape").

1169
Lest they should come – is all my fear
When sweet incarcerated here
c. 1870

(from 487)
But then His House – is but a Step –

(from 1760)
The very nearest Room

(from 788)
So fleet thou wert, when present –
So infinite – when gone –
An Orient's Apparition –
Remanded of the Morn –

The Height I recollect –
'Twas even with the Hills –
The Depth upon my soul was notched –
As Floods – on Whites of Wheels –

Those two stanzas convey his mercurial presence and the void in his absence and then give a visual recreation of his physical self ("The Height I recollect – / 'Twas even with the Hills –") which suggests that his shoulders were viewed as even with the hills seen outside her window, or analogous to them, perhaps in his embrace. [504]"You know that Portrait in the Moon –", describes Edward Dickinson's eyes as he lowered to her.
"I hide myself within my flower", refers to flowers she placed in his room, and in "fading from your Vase", "the flowering needs of her own sexuality are externalized";[157] in the last line of "Almost a loneliness.", she imputes is his.

903
I hide myself within my flower,
That fading from your Vase,
You, unsuspecting, feel for me –
Almost a loneliness.
c. 1864

In [707]"The Grace – Myself – might not obtain – " and in the second stanza of [682]"'Twould ease – a Butterfly – ", she again imagines herself as the flower. Contrarily she writes, [1579]"It would not know if it were spurned,". Then in a poem of five stanzas, a garland of devotion, [339]"I tend my flowers for thee – ".

Here, she waits in the parlor with the rest of the family for him to come home:

368
How sick – to wait – in any place – but thine –
I knew last night – when someone tried to twine –
Thinking – perhaps – that I looked tired – or alone –
Or breaking – almost – with unspoken pain –

And I turned – ducal –
That right – was thine –
One port – suffices for a Brig – like *mine* –

Ours be the tossing – wild though the sea –
Rather than a Mooring – unshared by thee.
Ours be the Cargo – *unladen – here* –
Rather than the *"spicy isles – "*
And thou – not there.
c. 1862

XXXIV

There exists a vantage point to closely peruse the poet at home: *Face to Face* provides a first-hand text by niece Martha, as though perched on a windowsill, sunny and fresh with affectionate intimacy. The only daughter of Emily Dickinson's brother Austin and sister-in-law Susan, Martha lived all of her young life next door to the Old Homestead at the Evergreens. In this memoir, she wrote vivid, detailed recollections of family and Amherst social life and particularly of her Aunt Emily, describing "the wide, old, upper hall of the mansion"[158] and then takes us with her: "The upper hall was my happiest hunting ground—Aunt Emily's room opened from it, and it was beyond the long arm of kitchen authority . . . . An open Franklin stove made a pretty blaze in cold weather, and a little writing table."[159]

At the poet's bedroom door, as further described by Martha, "She would stand looking down, one hand raised, thumb, and forefinger, closed on an imaginary key, and say, with a quick turn of her wrist, 'It's just a turn and freedom, Matty!'"[160]

There was an in-house correspondence: two versions of [494]"Going to Him! Happy letter!", [109]"By a flower – By a letter – ", and [334]"All the letters I can write". Here, plainspoken, the poet makes highly whimsical sense ([921]"If it had no pencil"). Martha designates the poet's bedroom a sanctum sanctorum, relating, "She read her letters here, never opening one until she was alone—not even so much as a note from a neighbor."[161] [636]"The Way I read a Letter's – this – ", which previews the extremity of the instruction to burn all of her correspondence at the end.

487
You love the Lord – you cannot see –
You write Him – everyday –
A little note – when you awake –
And further in the Day.

An Ample Letter – How you miss –
And would delight to see –
But then His House – is but a Step –
And Mine's – in Heaven – You see.
c. 1862

XXXV

Emily Dickinson maintained a brutal awareness of the conditions of living under her father's roof, and a clear knowledge of its terms, especially his anger ([348]"I dreaded that first Robin, so,") which may have been one reason he didn't let his mother stay. As a malevolent aspect of his authority one of the details noted by Habegger involves Edward Dickinson making a curious recommendation to wife Emily Norcross and daughter Emily that while they were in Boston to be sure to visit the Women's Asylum.[162] Edward Dickinson, "always so quick to raise the specter of 'insanity' or 'monomania,'"[163] considering it a disease, and was ostensibly an advocate, begs the question if that was because he could only watch as his father lay to waste his own future inheritance.[164] He ruled their lives, and here encoded, barely, was a harrowing means to leverage his control and illustrate the threat of being committed if he were crossed or inclined.

Emily Dickinson certainly had at twenty-two, her young fears, as she wrote in a letter to Sue Dickinson: "[and] I do fear sometimes that I must make a hospital for the hopelessly insane."[165] Several old Amherst families—the Strongs, distant cousins, the Montagues, and Boltwoods—did in fact have a child or sibling institutionalized in close by Northampton where an asylum had been established.[166]

Edward Dickinson was capable of doing just this through the same misogyny and legal expertise he brought to bear on a distraught woman who wished to divorce her husband because she was battered. He subpoenaed this woman's friends as witnesses to her being an emotionally unstable wife, by testifying in court that she cried continually, which she had done in turning to them for comfort.[167]

To be sure, the poet daughter, singled out by her father's lustful focus, had her own hidden, inestimable costs recorded in the following poem, reiterated in [1725]"I took one Draught of Life –".

580
I gave myself to Him –
And took Himself, for Pay,
The solemn contract of a Life
Was ratified, this way –

The Wealth might disappoint –
Myself a poorer prove
Than this great Purchaser suspect,
The Daily Own – of Love

Depreciate the Vision –
But till the Merchant buy –
Still Fable – in the Isles of Spice –
The subtle Cargoes – lie –

At least – 'tis Mutual – Risk –
Some – found it – Mutual Gain –
Sweet Debt of Life – Each Night to owe –
Insolvent – every Noon –
c. 1862

The process of editing *The Complete Poems* amply conveyed the all-consuming obsessive character of this relationship. Emily Dickinson's minds and moods, fractured or faceted, were a kaleidoscope of daily, if not hourly, shifts, ([765]"You constituted Time –"). As evident in many of her poems, the poet moved from one state of being to another—manic as in [364]"The Morning after Woe – "—at times herself incredulous, then proceeding variously through the degrees of belief, love, or ecstasy, and ever persistent, through the searing pain of two extremes of anger and powerlessness—always precipitated by his lordly and final decisions. In the following poem, the poet pleads that she is willing to assume responsibility, therefore blame, under threat of loss, not of relationship, but a pinion of sanity—her place at home—with him.

775
If Blame be my side – forfeit Me –
But doom me not to forfeit Thee –
To forfeit Thee? The very name
Is sentence from Belief – and Home –
c. 1863

As seen further, each of the following poems has a somber degree of its own, a
distinct message and tone, the first of which sounds consenting, hallowed, "Cashmere – or
Calvary – the same – / . . . / What Thou dost – is Delight – "; then a poem of rage, and
a secret, covered, kept forever; at the last, a righteous, and final, pithy, proud claim.

725
Where Thou art – that – is Home –
Cashmere – or Calvary – the same –
Degree – or Shame –
I scarce esteem Location's Name –
So I may Come –

What Thou dost – is Delight –
Bondage as Play – be sweet –
Imprisonment – Content –
And Sentence – Sacrament –
Just We two – meet –

Where Thou art not – is Woe –
Tho' Bands of Spices – row –
What Thou dost not – Despair –
Tho' Gabriel – praise me – Sir –
c. 1863

1737
Rearrange a "Wife's" affection!
When they dislocate my Brain!
Amputate my freckled Bosom!
Make me bearded like a man!

Blush, my spirit, in thy Fastness –
Blush, my unacknowledged clay –
Seven years of troth have taught thee
More than Wifehood ever may!

Love that never leaped its socket –
Trust entrenched in narrow pain –
Constancy thro' fire – awarded –
Anguish – bare of anodyne!

Burden – borne so far triumphant –
None suspect me of the crown,
For I wear the "Thorns" till *Sunset* –
Then – my Diadem put on.

Big my Secret but it's *bandaged* –
It will never get away
Till the Day its Weary Keeper
Leads it through the Grave to thee.
c. ?

1028
'Twas my one Glory –
Let it be
Remembered
I was owned of Thee –
c. 1865

This poem is reiterated in [349]"I had the Glory – that will do – ", which discloses an irredeemable loss. The last stanza of "Rearrange a "Wife's" affection!" intimates the record the poet intended by these poems for justice to be fully meted out by posterity, besides an immediate justice rendered by the poet for her own sake. The fantasies of self-mutilation, such as cutting off her breast, are symptomatic of those who have suffered sexual abuse, and subsequent self-loathing.[168]

Rage and Recrimination

XXXVI

1489
A Dimple in the Tomb
Makes that ferocious Room
A Home –
c. 1880

Twice it seems he ended this relationship, the last time likely being at the full cognitive maturity of a daughter ("A Giant – eye to eye with you,") who could inveigh by her words, at least in poetry, the challenge of a towering ego evident in the following poem.

275
Doubt Me! My Dim Companion!
Why, God, would be content
With but a fraction of the Life –
Poured thee, without a stint –
The whole of me – forever –
What more the Woman can,
Say quick, that I may dower thee
With last Delight I own!

It cannot be my Spirit –
For that was thine, before –
I ceded all of Dust I knew –
What Opulence the more

Had I – a freckled Maiden,
Whose farthest of Degree,
Was – that she might –
Some distant Heaven,
Dwell timidly, with thee!

Sift her, from Brow to Barefoot!
Strain till your last Surmise –
Drop, like a Tapestry, away,
Before the Fire's Eyes –
Winnow her finest fondness –
But hallow just the snow
Intact, in Everlasting flake –
Oh, Caviler, for you!
c. 1861

296
One Year ago – jots what?
God – spell the word! I – can't –
Was't Grace? Not that –
Was't Glory? That – will do –
Spell slower – Glory –

Such Anniversary shall be –
Sometimes – not often – in Eternity –
When farther Parted, than the Common Woe –
Look – feed upon each other's faces – so –
In doubtful meal, if it be possible
Their Banquet's true –

I tasted – careless – then –
I did not know the Wine
Came once a World – Did you?
Oh, had you told me so –
This Thirst would blister – easier – now –
You said it hurt you – most –
Mine – was an Acorn's Breast –
And could not know how fondness grew
In Shaggier Vest –
Perhaps – I couldn't –
But, had you looked in –
A Giant – eye to eye with you, had been –
No Acorn – then –

So – Twelve months ago –
We breathed –
Then dropped the Air –
Which bore it best?
Was this – the patientest –
Because it was a Child, you know –
And could not value – Air?

If to be "Elder" – mean most pain –
I'm old enough, today, I'm certain – then –
As old as thee – how soon?
One – Birthday more – or Ten?
Let me – choose!
Ah, Sir, None!
c. 1861

Reading "One Year ago – jots what? God – spell the word!" and in other poems—, [93]"Went up a year this evening!" [968]"Fitter to see Him, I may be" and [511]"If you were coming in the Fall,"—it is apparent that it was his time frame, of his devising and constraints, that she was clearly forced into. It seems there was at some point a moratorium of a year ("It don't sound so terrible – quite – as it did – ") within what could be the years' duration of this relationship ("Seven years of troth have taught thee") before the final time. This breaking off by Edward Dickinson is clearly inferred in word and intonation in the second stanza of [427]"I'll clutch – and clutch – ". He apparently raised the disparity of their ages as a wedge, which she belittles by the near taunt of these words: "You said it hurt you most – / Mine – was an Acorn's Breast – / And could not know how fondness grew / In Shaggier Vest – ". The substance, significance, of this is explicated in the poem [815]"The Luxury to apprehend".

These are long poems for Emily Dickinson, and they read as dramaturgy, such as "One Year – jots what?", in which imploring, angry, the poet asks rhetorically what is one year in their relationship, and then goes on to say, "I did not know the Wine / Came once a World – Did you?", lines which have their nexus in the poem [579]"I had been hungry, all the Years – ". [132]"I bring an unaccustomed wine" is like a postscript and [838]"Impossibility, like Wine" is also a part of this cluster.

Edward Dickinson presented another argument of the religious kind; [234]"You're right– "the way is narrow" – ", which his daughter vehemently and bitterly countered—on paper.

The endings were unilateral, as were the beginnings, triggering a dashed hope and anguish, anger, that can be read in a host of poems: [426]"It don't sound so terrible – quite – as it did – ", [49]"I never lost as much but twice," "Doubt Me! My Dim Companion!", and then the flailing "Kill your Balm – and its odors bless you – . . . Stab the Bird – ". The imagery of being aflutter, birdlike, in her breast, is also found in an early poem, [39]"It did not surprise me – ".

238
Kill your Balm – and its Odors bless you –
Bare your Jessamine – to the storm –
And she will fling her maddest perfume –
Haply – your Summer night to Charm –

Stab the Bird – that built in your bosom –
Oh, could you catch her last Refrain –
Bubble! "forgive" – "Some better" Bubble!
"Carol for Him when I am gone"!
c. 1861

In the histrionics of these poems, it is obvious that Emily Dickinson nears a dangerous emotional edge, precipitous and unbalancing, by an apparently sudden realization of how total and historic his control is and has been. The poet completely devolves to the childlike pathos and dire "If *He dissolve* – then – there is *nothing – more –* ". Then, finally, pathetically, she projects herself into "*His little Spaniel* – tell Him! – ", Carlos. She fancied the Dickinsons' spaniel as a liaison in the self-referential poem, [186]"What shall I do – it whimpers so – ", and with the dog as means or medium explicit in [1185]"A little Dog that wags his tail".

236
If *He dissolve* – then – there is *nothing – more –*
Eclipse – at *Midnight* –
It was *dark – before –*
Sunset – at *Easter*
Blindness – on the *Dawn –*
Faint Star of Bethlehem –
Gone down!

Would but some God – *inform* Him –
Or it be *too late*!
Say – that the pulse *just lisps* –
The *Chariots wait* –

———
78

Say – that a *little life* – for *His* –
Is *leaking* – *red* –
His little Spaniel – tell Him! –
Will He heed?
c. 1861

In this next poem, there is a complete surcease in the turbulence of the poet's angry desperation. Like an indicting one-woman Greek chorus, she gives herself the last word.

1280
The harm of Years is on him –
The infamy of Time –
Depose him like a Fashion
And give Dominion room.

Forget his Morning Forces –
The Glory of Decay –
Is a minuter Pageant
Than least Vitality.
c. 1873

Retrenchment and Recovery

XXXVII

"I cautious, scanned my little life –"

T he poems of this section I believe were created out of a motivation to not only unburden but to go back to the beginning—how the pain of her childhood particularly bore on her, baring personal truth, indelibly, unlike her tears.

With some ease one can piece together a fair likeness of Emily Dickinson as a child. In her poems, she was an observant child ([1149]"I noticed People disappeared"), and having a highly vocal curiosity, she "pondered original causes"[169] ([1258]"Who were "the Father and the Son""). The poem below, about control and, in this instance, the futility of parental exertion, constructs a metaphor based on her actual experience of being put in a "Closet," all because they liked her "still." There is a story in the niece's *Face to Face* when she tells her aunt of being shut up in a room by herself as a punishment: " . . . she confided to me, joyously, 'Matty, child, no one could ever punish a Dickinson by shutting her up alone.'"[170]

613
They shut me up in Prose –
As when a little Girl
They put me in the Closet –
Because they liked me "still" –

Still! Could themself have peeped –
And seen my Brain – go round –
They might as wise have lodged a Bird
For Treason – in the Pound –

Himself has but to will
And easy as a Star
Abolish his Captivity –
And laugh – No more have I –
c. 1862

Their controlling issues outweighing the caring ones, show that by parental lights, little Emily, besides precocious, was irrepressible, and possessed an overabundance of spirit, constant inquiry, and summations.

An ecstatic child—then the poet—who wrote [1118]"Exhilaration is the Breeze", [1640]"Take all away from me, but leave me Ecstasy," and the famously anthologized [214]"I taste a liquor never brewed – " with each of the poems embodying what Emily Dickinson could have alluded to in a letter to Thomas Wentworth Higginson (co-editor of her 1890 posthumous publication): "I always ran Home to Awe when a child, if anything befell me, He was an awful Mother, but I liked him better than none."[171] These oft-quoted words indicate a quick and early formation in her powers of observation and acute response to the natural world (those outdoor objects watched closely as a child, in the cozy environ of yard and field), a meaning greatly at odds with the usual interpretation of this missive implying criticism of her mother's failure of nurturance. Surely what could be underlying her meaning or sense of "Awe" is a statement also made to Higginson in a letter saying that nature induces "a palsy . . . the Verses just relieve". (With the logicality of feeling and palsy as a product of an "awful Mother",[172] her verse-making is again a refuge and respite.)

The "Prose" was indoors—her father's downstairs library books kept in a floor-to-ceiling bookcase, shelf upon shelf of complete histories or works, English and American tomes (of the Revolution, Alexander Hamilton, Thomas Jefferson, John Adams), British essayists, and many "Travels," just leaving room for Shakespeare in eight volumes, Byron, and other lesser-known English poets. Besides these shelves, there were also myriad periodicals the Dickinsons received.

1534
Society for me my misery
Since Gift of Thee –
c. 1881

These two lines seem to mean that her father's company alone is pleasurable ([720]"No Prisoner be – "), although it could also mean sardonically that misery is society accompanied by shame. However any interpretation would indicate a homebound creature. Besides shut up in prose, home was a place where she experienced imprisonment ([1334]"How soft this Prison is" and [128]"Bring me the sunset in a cup,") and a need to escape, as described in [1347]"Escape is such a thankful Word" and in the sixth stanza of [652]"A Prison gets to be a friend – ", then the cryptic [1166]"Of Paul and Silas it is said", each a sample of an array of forms of incarceration and liberty thematic in her poetry. As an image, the "House" is a prosaic construct, the Old Homestead—its pre-eminence always in the soul of the Dickinson family—often manifest in the poetry of their child and grandchild, felt in [657]"I dwell in Possibility – ", and [1119]"Paradise is that old mansion". (Aunt Catherine in 1835 wrote her parents in Ohio, "I never saw any place half so beautiful as our own home.")[173] Then home in a late poem becomes a magical imprisonment, perhaps nostalgic: [1601]"Of God we ask one favor,".

XXXVIII

When I read "It would have starved a Gnat – " the origins of her pain was clearly recognizable, a template of pain, a sense of non-existence, all encompassing, an effect of powerlessness, suspended, over a tremendous gap in nurturance.

612
It would have starved a Gnat –
To live so small as I –
And yet I was a living child –
With Food's necessity

Upon me – like a Claw –
I could no more remove
Than I could coax a Leech away –
Or make a Dragon – move –

Nor like the Gnat – had I –
The privilege to fly
And seek a Dinner for myself –
How mightier He – than I –

Nor like Himself – the Art
Upon the Window Pane
To gad my little Being out –
And not begin – again –
c. 1862

Childhood pain as a premise for an unsentimental poem was completely outside nineteenth century poetic convention and was created by Emily Dickinson in an utterly original, new voice. (The other American original, Walt Whitman in his *Leaves of Grass*, was as loquacious as hers was laconic, both in a spoken vernacular. Robert Bly in his *American Poetry, Wildness and Domesticity*, speaks of each of these poets with revelatory authority.)

Her exact and trusting disclosures ("To live so small as I – ") prompted me to look for other poems that might have been written about the poet's first traces of pain. In the few that were written, she was able to convey the pathways of terror opened to her very early in life, and without the poet's self-pity, we are allowed to feel for ourselves what it was like 'To live so small'. (The one exception to this mode is [588]"I cried at Pity – not at Pain – " where the first stanza declares the poet's true feeling, and then feeling unvalued as a child not made of gold, she dissociates, spinning-like, in stanzas to the end of the poem.)

The next poem from a mature perspective, "I groped for him", vouches that only a sacramental, preordained source, could be considered nourishing sustenance, limpid in contrast to "It would have starved a Gnat – ". Another poem using the very same imagery is [1269]"I worked for chaff and earning Wheat", reportorial and reflective of adult experience.

1555
I groped for him before I knew
With solemn nameless need
All other bounty sudden chaff
For this foreshadowed Food
Which others taste and spurn and sneer –
Though I within suppose
That consecrated it could be
The only Food that grows
c. 1882

Still another, [1297]"Go slow, my soul, to feed thy self", repeats the imagery of nourishment-satiation, from starvation and savoring his coming, to receiving a "Kiss"—for which she sold her soul's salvation. [1282]"Art thou the thing I wanted?" claims that now older she has evolved to the tip of abstinence waiting for him.

It is in [1010]"Up Life's Hill with my little Bundle" that she is telling us her sense of isolation within her family and the degree to which she felt homeless—the price of the relationship with her father—to be outside of that family circle, irregular, if not broken, as it was. Further thinking upon her childhood's pain can be read in [1021]"Far from Love the Heavenly Father". [690]"Victory comes late – " describes the cold and starvation and is a summation of being loved-starved.

The poet replays the frozen image, equating food with love, but is high-minded, remonstrative and resigned.

Below, "'Tis true – They shut me in the Cold – " discloses using the cold as punishment, a controlling device, possibly setting the child in a chilly anteroom (common in the colder climes). After telling on her parents with "Forgive Them – Even as Myself", she then expresses loyalty. (Despite the pain of their abuse, children are likely to be protective of parents.)

538
'Tis true – They shut me in the Cold –
But then – Themselves were warm
And could not know the feeling 'twas –
Forget it – Lord – of Them –

Let not my Witness hinder Them
In Heavenly esteem –
No Paradise could be – Conferred
Through Their beloved Blame –

The Harm They did – was short – And since
Myself – who bore it – do –
Forgive Them – Even as Myself –
Or else – forgive not me –
c. 1862

Then the following poem reveals once more that Emily Dickinson was subjected to the cold as behavior modification, meant this time to break her of a lisp. She teases them with feigning relapse, and then says they will in hindsight see her stoic and sweet, but when they call her indoors frozen, she will be unable to "thank Them for the Ice".

874
They won't frown always – some sweet Day
When I forget to tease –
They'll recollect how cold I looked
And how I just said "Please."

Then They will hasten to the Door
To call the little Girl
Who cannot thank Them for the Ice
That filled the lisping full.
c. 1864

XXXIX

After her father's death, in the last years, [1260]"Because that you are going", Emily Dickinson did not venture beyond the hedge, and her niece tells us, "[But] at the tall pine on the driveway she would stop, leaving me with the same gentle promise, 'Another night dear.'"[174] Her bedroom, "A sort of lookout, too, it had become, from which she could 'observe the earth beneath'"[175] or drop gingerbread in baskets to neighborhood children—a place that the poet was forced to forfeit, almost to its ground—a world she then drew to herself through the windows of the Old Homestead, and viewed through the eyes of others, their reports, friends or family, with the accompaniments of gifts, music, and attention: [1391]"They might not need me – yet they might – ". Toward the end of her life, visitors were observed or spoken with through a veil of dimness, a downstairs door left ajar like a long taper candle on the outer world of a foyer.[176] "In summer we watched the orioles outside," Martha remembered,

> or the cherries ripening—or the bees—or a random hummingbird at the honeysuckle by the east window where her little writing-table stood; for in Aunt Emily's time there were three tall cherry trees in a line just bordering the flagstone walk at the east side of the house, and all the way down to the garden, plum and pear trees, very white and garlandly in the spring. Where the slope in the grass came, to the lower terrace, the orchard began, with apple blossoms for Whit-Sunday, which we called 'White-Sunday,' . . . [177]

This same view from "the slope" onward is easily beheld in her aunt Emily's poem below.

375
The Angle of a Landscape –
That every time I wake –
Between my Curtain and the Wall
Upon an ample Crack –

Like a Venetian – waiting –
Accosts my open eye –
Is just a Bough of Apples –
Held slanting, in the Sky –

The Pattern of a Chimney –
The Forehead of a Hill –

Sometimes – a Vane's Forefinger –
But that's – Occasional –

The Seasons – shift – my Picture –
Upon my Emerald Bough,
I wake – to find no – Emeralds –
Then – Diamonds – which the Snow

From Polar Caskets – fetched me –
The Chimney – and the Hill –
And just the Steeple's finger –
These – never stir at all –
c. 1862

The picturesque description by Martha Dickinson Bianchi, a lush view shared by niece and aunt from the bedroom window, offers a contrasting and unique comparison to the faceted and geometric jewel-like stanzas of "The Angle of a Landscape – ", referring to a larger world as far as Venice, with quilt-like depictions of the changing seasons and the stationary steeple. Similarly, just as niece Martha could not ever see a branch of red apples as a Venetian bedecked in rubies, or "Polar Caskets", it was as impossible for her being a child to espy the facade, shifts of scenes surrounding her aunt, let alone the dramatis personae—aunt, grandfather—and their kind of relationship of course inconceivable. Martha grown up, however, did write later in both her naiveté and ignorance, "Emily, most of all, would have been appalled to realize her little momentary elfish fantasies about him were ever to be taken literally and solemnly examined for posterity by aliens in spirit as in comprehension."[178] This recalls the left-handed denial in Richard Chase's study *Emily Dickinson* that Edward Dickinson was not "the lover-in-disguise he is sometimes assumed to be."

663
Again – his voice is at the door –
I feel the old *Degree* –
I hear him ask the servant
For such an one – as me –

I take a *flower* – as I go –
My face to *justify* –
He never *saw* me – *in this life* –
I might *surprise* his eye!

I cross the Hall with *mingled* steps –
I – silent – pass the door –
I look on all this world *contains* –
Just his face – nothing more!

We talk in *careless* – and in *toss* –
A kind of *plummet* strain –
Each – sounding – shyly –
Just – how – deep –
The *other's* one – had been –

We *walk* – I leave my Dog – at home –
A *tender* – *thoughtful* Moon
Goes with us – just a little way –
And – then – we are *alone* –

Alone – if *Angels* are "alone" –
First time they *try* the sky!
Alone – if those "veiled faces" – be –
We cannot *count* – on High!

I'd give – to live that hour – *again* –
The *purple* – *in my Vein* –
But *He* must *count the drops* – *himself* –
My price for *every stain*!
c. 1862

RECLAMATION AND RESOLVE

XL

1732
My life closed twice before its close –
It yet remains to see
If Immortality unveil
A third event to me.

So huge, so hopeless to conceive
As these that twice befell.
Parting is all we know of heaven,
And all we need of hell.
c. ?

The following poem, a retrospective, pensive soliloquy, mainly recapitulates a relationship that is well over. First to say, "Difference – had begun – Many a bitterness had been – ", Emily Dickinson proceeds to affirm her happiness that had been complete "I put my pleasure all about – ", then vanquished without the merest vestige of its "moment of Brocade". "Such bliss – had I – for all the years – / 'Twould give an easier pain – " insinuates that the poet had most likely long realized the excessive, powerless nature of her pain, from which she could only retreat or to which she could only succumb. Her moment of final clarity comes "When – suddenly – my Riches shrank – / A Goblin – drank my Dew – ", and the empty glass sings, the poet keens,—time, texture and tincture—gone.

430

It would never be Common – more – I said –
Difference – had begun –
Many a bitterness – had been –
But that old sort – was done –

Or – if it sometime – showed – as 'twill –
Upon the Downiest – Morn –
Such bliss – had I – for all the years –
'Twould give an Easier – pain –

I'd so much joy – I told it – Red –
Upon my simple Cheek –
I felt it publish – in my Eye –
'Twas needless – any speak –

I walked – as wings – my body bore –
The feet – I former used –
Unnecessary – now to me –
As boots – would be – to Birds –

I put my pleasure all abroad –
I dealt a word of Gold
To every Creature – that I met –
And Dowered – all the World –

When – suddenly – my Riches shrank –
A Goblin – drank my Dew –
My Palaces – dropped tenantless –
Myself – was beggared – too –

I clutched at sounds –
I groped at shapes –
I touched the tops of Films –
I felt the Wilderness roll back
Along my Golden lines –

The Sackcloth – hangs upon the nail –
The Frock I used to wear –
But where my moment of Brocade –
My – drop – of India?
c. 1862

The following poem establishes a plane of awareness without self, but which is nonetheless alive and enduring in her poetry, "Who wrought Carrara in me / And chiselled all my tune".

1046
I've dropped my Brain – My Soul is numb –
The Veins that used to run
Stop palsied – 'tis Paralysis
Done perfecter on stone

Vitality is Carved and cool.
My nerve in Marble lies –
A Breathing Woman
Yesterday – Endowed with Paradise.

Not dumb – I had a sort that moved –
A Sense that smote and stirred –
Instincts for Dance – a caper part –
An Aptitude for Bird –

Who wrought Carrara in me
And chiselled all my tune
Were it a Witchcraft – were it Death –
I've still a chance to strain

To Being, somewhere – Motion – Breath –
Though Centuries beyond,
And every limit a Decade –
I'll shiver, satisfied.
c. 1865

Emily Dickinson ("Not dumb – I had a sort that moved – / A Sense that smote and stirred – / Instincts for Dance – a caper part – / An Aptitude for Bird – ") gives us a self-portrait—autonomous as only she could know to delineate—to share with posterity. The place of the immortals where she saw Emily Brönte, in her hymn of praise "Oh what an afternoon for Heaven, / When "Brönte" entered there!" It is in complete accord with the image recollected by her niece Martha of both the poet's appearance and manner:

> . . . her dark expressive eyes with their tint of bronze, and Titian hair set
> off by white skin, . . . parted low on her brow, drooping loosely in thick

strands to a coil at the back of her neck . . . . She often moved about in a sort of reverie of her own flitting always and quick as a trout if disturbed. Her low-pitched voice was the instrument of an unconscious artist, almost husky at times of intensity . . . . [179]

It was a fleet behavior reminiscent of Emily Brönte, who at the sight of the butcher boy delivering at Haworth would, like a bird, disappear panicked.[180]

Emily Dickinson's transcendence of tragedy ("When One has given up One's life") was "tripartite":[181] first, in the act of surviving trauma—the poem the province of the painful truth—reaffirming a "feminine inviolability,"[182] and then finding herself deluded but coming to a realization of cylindrical clarity, and finally the "solitary splendor",[183] of a bright epiphany, progressively marked in the poems she would not at the end burn like her letters ([1022]"I knew that I had gained"). If it be imagined that transcendence is without bumpiness, her poems [1013]"Too scanty 'twas to die for you," and [1017]"To die – without the Dying" completely dispense of this notion. Enlightenment for the poet, (also produced of hardy self-actualization [384]"No Rack can torture me – "), was when she knew she had written poetry that could last to be read ([1275]"The Spider as an Artist"). She then could let go of the pain of sacrifice demanded by the supremacy of her father's needs and bring down the lead mirror of an unpublished poet. Besides the lines from the previous poem, "I've still a chance to strain / To Being somewhere – Motion – Breath – / Though Centuries beyond," she wrote, [431]"Me – come! My dazzled face", describing a veritable Tahiti of renown, as well as a subdued, succinct [713]"Fame of Myself, to justify,".

XLI

Along with her continued practice as a poet ([843]"I made slow Riches but my Gain"), there was a powerful inference in the behavior of a friend to convey to Emily Dickinson the possibility of finding an appreciative readership as a published poet. Only a great dramatist could have believably contrived the circumstances, synchronicity, for a Helen Hunt Jackson born in Amherst the same year as the poet, to be a girlhood acquaintance, and then years later to have their paths cross, with the high-spirited western writer intimately intervening upon the poet's hidden writing life. By pure happenstance—the highest rung glistening in this cloud of synchronicity—Jackson, recently widowed and tragically childless in 1865, returned east to Newport, Rhode Island, and where she took up lodging in the same boarding house as Colonel Higginson, the very same Thomas Wentworth whom Emily Dickinson had chosen as mentor, and who then showed her poems to Jackson, this long-ago Amherst connection.[184] (Higginson had also encouraged and advised Jackson as a new writer.)

Helen Hunt Jackson, who became author of the folkloric *Ramona* and advocate for the Mission Indians of the San Gabriel valley in Southern California, progressively exemplifying "life is a reciprocal process,"[185] left home early on and proceeded to live a life opposite of the poet's—published, twice married, a mother, writing in the west—and beseeched her friend Emily to publish. [67]"Success is counted sweetest" was one of two published through Helen Hunt Jackson in her 1878 volume *A Masque of Poets*.[186] (The poet did see a small handful of her poems in print in her lifetime, though all were published without her name. *The Springfield Republican*, edited by friend Samuel Bowles, printed five, and in February and March 1864, three appeared in *Drum Beat*, a Brooklyn paper with the purpose of raising money for medical care for Union soldiers, and one in the *Brooklyn Daily Union*.[187])

Believing in the beauty and worth of Emily Dickinson's poetry, and presumably on a friend's errand to express this, Jackson showed up at the poet's doorstep of the Old Homestead, and perhaps it was the time in October, 1878,[188] when Helen Hunt came to offer her willingness to make submissions, disguised for the poet in her handwriting.[189] In any event, it was a scene of high drama, as depicted by her agog niece Martha:

> [The] memory is that of a span of horses being walked up and down before the house while Helen Hunt went inside . . . . Many times the driver turned them around at the same tree, walked them as far as our own front gate, and turned them around again, . . . At last, after an hour or more, a figure appeared, [and] sprang into the waiting carriage, ... [190]

The clattering sashay, rare fanfare, before the poet's front steps gave, it could seem, the final flourish to Helen Hunt Jackson's avowed admiration. It could be also that this visitor saw Edward Dickinson's death as the end of paternal entrapment for her friend and wanted Emily Dickinson to confront its surviving pattern as a sequestered poet, perhaps prompting [1513]"Go traveling with us!". Also, this may have been the occasion for the poet in 1879 to write [1473]"We talked with each other about each other"—especially of that which remained unsaid.

XLII

It is in the last stanza of "I got so I could take his name – " where the poet describes "My Business, with the Cloud," and the creation of poems subsuming her pain ("It care, in some remoter way, For so minute affair / as Misery – "), morally wise, Emily Dickinson relegates a lifetime of pain. [584]"It ceased to hurt me, though so slow".

293
I got so I could take his name –
Without – Tremendous gain –
That Stop-sensation – on my Soul –
And Thunder – in the Room –

I got so I could walk across
That Angle in the floor,
Where he turned so, and I turned – how –
And all our Sinew tore –

I got so I could stir the Box –
In which his letters grew
Without that forcing, in my breath –
As Staples – driven through –

Could dimly recollect a Grace –
I think, they call it "God" –
Renowned to ease Extremity –
When Formula, had failed –

And shape my Hands –
Petition's way,
Tho' ignorant of a word
That Ordination – utters –

My Business, with the Cloud,
If any Power behind it, be,
Not subject to Despair –
It care, in some remoter way,
For so minute affair
As Misery –
Itself, too vast, for interrupting – more –
c. 1861

From "Cloud" level, we may imagine a distant time in the arboretum of the Old Homestead, (and as once happened) the twin vision of Emily Dickinson in white and a white butterfly—an ecstatic presence, surprise emergence—([129]"Cocoon above! Cocoon below!"), and share in the recognition of the autonomy, exquisite air, Emily Dickinson found on wings of poetry, ([1099]"My Cocoon tightens – Colors tease – "), both poet and butterfly in the thrall of delight and release—she perhaps, with ethereal irony, Marion Woodman's "Conscious Virgin" of *The Maiden King*.

Afterword

The Monarch butterfly, ubiquitous in her poetry and whose winged brilliance she once saw far down a torrid, dusty road, just may be [1766]"Those final Creatures, – who they are – " known of her summers imbued of heart and warmth, paused for the ages. Six editions and every copy sold from the first *Poems* in 1890, Samuel G. Ward, Transcendentalist and writer for the *Dial*, wrote to Higginson (who showed it to Mabel Todd), "She may become world famous, or she may never get out of New England."

In 1886 Westinghouse electrified for two weeks the small village of Great Barrington of Western Massachusetts; and Sewall the biographer in his first volume wrote "the Dickinsons were pure stock, without even a wife in seven generations from outside New England," that was until 1903 when niece Martha Bianchi married Alexander an Italian count. It is Martha's descriptions of how Aunt Emily's auburn hair nestled at the back of her neck, bedeviled sister Vinnie with her "pussies", that "droll" was her favorite word, and she played wildly in the middle of the night of The Old Homestead her own piano compositions, that I found most endearing, imagining, "quick as a trout", a luminous shadow, the diminutive figure in a white dress—not as "'Her Columnar Self'", a New England Puritan, poet of pain—but herself, humbled by pleasure.

Marne Carmean   West Hollywood, California   September, 2007

ENDNOTES

1. There is an additional number of poems not included in the Johnson edition with an adjusted total of 1,789 read in a marathon reading honoring National Poetry Month at the Emily Dickinson Museum, (The Old Homestead) April 2006.
2. Weil, *Inside Incest*, 19.
3. Chase, *Emily Dickinson*, 11.
4. Wolff, *Emily Dickinson*, xix.
5. Wolff xix.
6. Woodman, *Addiction to Perfection*, 136.
7. Woodman 136.
8. Woodman 136.
9. Woodman 137.
10. Woodman 137.
11. What is now called the Emily Dickinson Museum, as of the restoration of the Homestead's exterior carpentry and masonry completed in the fall of 2004.
12. Kat Ward, discussion, Los Angeles, California, 1999.
13. Morison, *The Oxford History of American People*, 66.
14. Tindall, *America: A Narrative History*, 61.
15. Morison 65.
16. Morison 71-72.
17. Belloc, "The South Country," *An Anthology of Recent Poetry*, 39.
18. Hawkes, *The World of the Past*, 273·
19. Bianchi, *The Life and Letters of Emily Dickinson*, 5.
20. Morison 65.
21. Morison 67.
22. Sewall, *The Life of Emily Dickinson*, 18·
23. Sewall 18.
24. Habegger, *My Wars Are Laid Away in Books*, 5.

25. Morison 71. By an act in 1647 of the Bay Colony, every town of a hundred families or more was required to set up a grammar school based on the English model, which by today's standards would amount to a secondary education, with the study of Greek and Latin grammar.

26. Sewall 37, Habegger 9. Samuel Fowler Dickinson created educational opportunities for his daughters.

27. Sewall 19.

28. Sewall 19.

29. Sewall 20.

30. Sewall 24.

31. Sewall 24.

32. Sewall 25.

33. Sewall 38, n. 11.

34. Habegger 339.

35. Sewall 42. A long verse (57 quatrains) by Elizabeth Dickinson Currier for an 1883 family reunion celebrating the mark and mien of the men and women of the Dickinson family, in this instance her father Samuel's mother and father, grandparents Nathan Jr. and Esther, marvelously biographical.

36. Habegger 628.

37. Habegger 57.

38. Habegger 21.

39. Habegger 19.

40. Sewall 19.

41. Sewall 41 n. 12 enumerates poems about Samuel Fowler Dickinson by his granddaughter.

42. Sewall 19.

43. Sewall 41: "[Samuel Fowler Dickinson] who stood in the forefront in the Amherst of his generation; a fine scholar; a lawyer of distinction and wide practice; a man of rare public spirit, the highest moral purpose, and unflagging zeal", November 7, 1889. 307, n. 41.

44. Sewall 20.

45. Sewall 18.

46. Wolff 16, 17. See also Tindall 109 - 110.

47. Habegger 12.

48. Habegger 9. See also Wolff 14: " . . . bedchambers the size of sitting rooms. Indeed, the residents of Amherst would have been justified in surmising that the house was a gracious but explicit assertion of money and success."

49. Sewall 41.

50. Tindall 261.

51. Wolff 13.

52. Van Doren, *The Great Rehearsal*, 198. " . . . People, I say, took up arms, and then, if you went to speak to them, you had the musket of death presented to your breast . . . so that you see that anarchy leads to tyranny, . . . " Jonathan Smith of Lanesboro in Berkshire County speaking January 25, 1788, at the Federal Convention in Massachusetts for the ratification of the Constitution.

53. Tindall 109.

54. The Compact Edition of the Oxford English Dictionary, 586, 1101.

55. Sewall 22. "Perry Miller's note on the 'Protestant ethic[:] No activity is outside the holy purpose of the overarching covenant.'"

56. Wainright, "Jonathan Edwards," np. "They are not indeed cut off from all the charity of God's people, for all men ought to be the objects of their love. But I speak of the brotherly charity due to visible saints." See also Tindall 110.

57. Wainright np.

58. Morison 151.

59. Wainwright np.

60. Sewall 30.

61. Sewall 29.

62. Sewall 34, n. 9.

63. Chase 9.

64. Habegger 16.

65. Habegger 21.

66. Sewall 33.

67. Patricia Behr Whitten, discussion, Silver Lake, Los Angeles, 1982.

68. Wolff 6.

69. Habegger 105.

70. Wolff 124.

71. Wolff 29-31.

72. Habegger 338-340.

73. Wolff 92, 564.

74. Wolff 78-79, 99.

75. Wolff 103

76. Habegger 239.

77. Wolff 166.

78. Habegger 261.

79. Wolff 492.

80. Habegger 330-333.

81. Habegger 317.

82. Habegger 331-334.

83. Wolff 510.

84. Habegger 330.

85. Habegger 333.
86. Wolff, 552 n. 45, 575 n. 61. See also 410: " . . . for in her own life, Emily Dickinson consistently construed the Word not as a supplement to ordinary human relationships, but as an alternative to them."
87. Habegger 485.
88. Habegger 486.
89. Habegger 453.
90. Habegger 483-484.
91. Wolff 167, 492 - 493.
92. Habegger 342.
93. Habegger 597-598.
94. Bianchi, *Emily Dickinson Face to Face*, 7.
95. Wolff 3.
96. Habegger 22.
97. Sewall 57.
98. Sewall 55.
99. Habegger 88.
100. Habegger 346.
101. Habegger 560.
102. Rodgers, *The Work Ethic in Industrial America*, 22.
103. Habegger 505.
104. Habegger 346.
105. Habegger 563-564.
106. Bianchi, *Emily Dickinson Face to Face*, 22.
107. Sewall 56.
108. Habegger 115.
109. Wolff 410.
110. Bianchi, *The Life and Letters of Emily Dickinson*, 8.
111. Bianchi, *Emily Dickinson Face to Face*, 86.
112. Bianchi, *Emily Dickinson Face to Face*, 86.
113. Morison 71.
114. Chase 9.
115. Habegger 344. See also Wolff 134.
116. Sewall 250.
117. Bianchi, *Emily Dickinson Face to Face*, 67.
118. Wolff 108.
119. Wolff 58.
120. Habegger 63. See also 503: Margaret Mahler, a long time housekeeper, was reluctant to work for the Dickinsons because there wasn't enough to do and she found the home strange. Edward Dickinson to keep her in his employ threatened that if she didn't work for him she would not work for any of the Dickinsons.

121. Wolff 64, 501. See also Habegger 565.
122. Bianchi, *The Life and Letters of Emily Dickinson*, 9.
123. Habegger 565.
124. Habegger 136, 411, between April, 1859 and November, 1862, the poet on six occasions was legal witness to her father's real estate transactions.
125. Habegger 344.
126. Habegger 82.
127. Bianchi, *Emily Dickinson Face to Face*, 85.
128. Bianchi, *The Life and Letters of Emily Dickinson*, 8-9.
129. Habegger 27. The quote is a statement by the principal of the academy in Monson and can perhaps be found in Daybook no. 11, Monson Historical Society.
130. Wolff 501.
131. Wolff 554 n.63.
132. Habegger 502.
133. Habegger 390.
134. Habegger 454.
135. Habegger 559.
136. Habegger 251-252 See also Sewall 44.
137. Wolff 118.
138. Sewall 62.
139. Sewall 62.
140. Sewall 63.
141. Sewall 65, f.8.
142. Sewall 59.
143. Sewall 73.
144. Habegger 339.
145. Habegger 563.
146. Sewall 50.
147. MacKinnon, Catharine, A. *Only Words*, 77.
148. Wolff 64.
149. Habegger 353.
150. Wolff 176.
151. Wolff 547-548, n. 4.
152. Wolff 546, n. 51 See also 35.
153. Wolff 35.
154. Anne Kennedy, discussion, Laurel Canyon, Los Angeles, 1969.
155. Bianchi, *Emily Dickinson Face to Face*, 21-22.
156. Wolff 33. See also Richard B. Sewall, ed. pp. 70-71. *The Lyman Letters: New Light on Emily Dickinson and Her Family*.
157. Linda DeVore, discussion, Lutz, Florida, 1998.
158. Bianchi, *Emily Dickinson Face to Face*, 10-11.

159. Bianchi, *Emily Dickinson Face to Face*, 65-66.
160. Bianchi, *Emily Dickinson Face to Face*, 66.
161. Bianchi, *Emily Dickinson Face to Face*, 66.
162. Habegger 176.
163. Habegger 411.
164. Habegger 13.
165. Habegger 410.
166. Habegger 715, n. 411.
167. Habegger 288.
168. Perriman, Wendy, K. *A Wounded Deer: The Effects of Incest on the Life and Poetry of Emily Dickinson*, x. E. Sue Blume, L.C. S.W., The Incest Survivors' Aftereffects Checklist. (Number seven, out of thirty-seven, concerning self-mutilation and other self-harming behaviors.)
169. Anne Kennedy, discussion, Laurel Canyon, Los Angeles, 1969.
170. Bianchi, *Emily Dickinson Face to Face*, 86-77.
171. Habegger 117.
172. Habegger 455.
173. Sewall 38.
174. Bianchi, *Emily Dickinson Face to Face*, 66.
175. Bianchi, *Emily Dickinson Face to Face*, 10-11.
176. Wolff 510. See also Habegger 611.
177. Bianchi, *Emily Dickinson Face to Face*, 4.
178. Bianchi, *Emily Dickinson Face to Face*, 105.
179. Bianchi, *Emily Dickinson Face to Face*, 16-18.
180. Habegger 605.
181. Cathleen Wells, discussion, Laurel Canyon, Los Angeles, 1979.
182. Anne Kennedy, discussion, Laurel Canyon, Los Angeles, 1962.
183. Anne Kennedy, discussion, Laurel Canyon, Los Angeles, 1965.
184. Habegger 555.
185. Linda Weider, discussion, West Hollywood, California, 1977.
186. Habegger 559.
187. Habegger 402.
188. Wolff 509.
189. Habegger 558.
190. Bianchi, *Emily Dickinson Face to Face*, 35-36. See also Wolff 555-556

Indices of Images and Ideas

---

i

The Complete Poems of Emily Dickinson, edited by Thomas H. Johnson, serves as the primary source for this book and is the reference for the following indices of images and ideas. These are the first lines of poems in my book and the first lines of poems not included, yet which are germane, having the same ideas and images, and that may in their turn serve the reader to confirm (or not) the specific consistencies, constancies, discovered in the aggregate sense of her poetry.

A tapestry of poetry by the doomed, redeemed daughter of Edward Dickinson has a consistent, connotative, value in the brilliant hues and agonizing shadows of this father-daughter relationship. These indices serve to make available to the reader nearly all of those words of special meaning by which the poet told the truth of her being, apprised by garnering the reiterations (gathering, counting after a fashion) the number of times that a word or an image and metaphor were repeated, as often as the poet felt a need to formulate again her reassertions. A glittering concordance arose by untwisting strands of multicolored threads of entwined metaphor, symbol, pearly detail ("thill of bee"), forming clusters revealing the poems that tell of the real interior of this poet's life, by reiterating ideas and images ("altered echoes"), resonant and thematically rich.

Emily Dickinson's poems, are exquisite, variegated, explorations of the truth created for the sake of comprehension, crystallization, and closure, offered to the sacred archives of poetry.

ii

To ease the inquiries of the reader, the poems are in four groups: In the first two groups I have italicized the first lines of the poems present in the book

---

103

and separating by a space those poems whose first lines only have been utilized. Again dropping a space, the third group, and without italics, are the first lines of poems that are pertinent to this relationship but not included in the book. The last group, dropped by a space and again without italics, are first lines of poems having the same word or a similar idea but devoid of meaning relevant to this father-daughter relationship. For simplicity referring to the Indices I have maintained an alphabetical order and a chronological one using Johnson's poem numbers.

iii

These indices encompass most of the poems revealing the poet's relationship with her father, mainly reactive, to her father (dispositions, descriptions, and dynamics of that relationship), early and late, if not posthumously. The poet's sexuality preternaturally exploited, the delectable feelings, remained hers, a self-enjoyment that permeates numerous poems here, especially those of the months of May and June, seasons of yearning beginning in February ("till my heart is red as February and purple as March"), through her hoped-for prolonged summer. A book of poems could be made of her summers.

There are any number of words and images, ideas, that are not grouped and brought into the indices which clearly had special meaning to Emily Dickinson, as they are ubiquitous in her poetry: butterfly, bee, brooks and seas, eclipse, spice, to name a few. There are surely a few poems that categorically ought to have been indexed, but as the poems of Emily's lisp, they may have slipped through the rake.

iv

Finally, there is a capacious summation in the whole of *The Complete Poems of Emily Dickinson* that can be viewed in the darkly rugged philosophy and spiritual light of Emily Dickinson's sensibilities, pinnacles of mortification and majesty, which like her own shining tents, envelope her poetry and the reader, [1097]"Dew – is the Freshet in the Grass –".

INDICES

ANGER

***

ANGUISH

***

APPALLING

ATOMS

***

BOMB

***

***

BRIDE

271   *A solemn thing – it was – I said –*
300   *"Morning" – means "Milking"- to the Farmer –*
473   *I am ashamed – I hide –*
493   *The World – stands – solemner – to me –*
518   *Her sweet Weight on my Heart a Night*
1072   *Title divine – is mine!*
1496   *All that I do*

1   *Oh the Earth was made for lovers, for damsel, and hopeless swain,*
586   *We talked as Girls do –*
625   *'Twas a long Parting – but the time*
1257   *Dominion lasts until obtained –*

649   Her Sweet turn to leave the Homestead
817   Given in Marriage unto Thee
1756   'Twas here my summer paused

830   To this World she returned.
1404   March is the Month of Expectation.
1620   Circumference thou Bride of Awe

CALVARY

725   *Where Thou art – that – is Home –*

322   *There came a Day at Summer's full,*
364   *The Morning after Woe –*
549   *That I did always love*

***

126   To fight aloud, is very brave –
561   I measure every Grief I meet
577   If I may have it, when it's dead,
1432   Spurn the temerity –

CARLO & KATIE

***

***

CHILD, LITTLE GIRL, SCHOOL MOTIF

CROWNS

COCHINEAL

COCOON

COLD, FREEZING, POLAR

DAISY

***

DEGREE

***

DOLLIE

***

***

DIMPLES

***

EMILY'S LISP

538   *'Tis true – They shut me in the Cold –*
874   *They won't frown always – some sweet Day*

50   *I haven't told my garden yet –*
399   *A House upon the Height –*
877   *Each Scar I'll keep for Him*
1094 *Themself are all I have –*   The poet enunciates
                                            the lisp in the diction
                                            of her poems.

1409 *Could mortal lip divine*   An adult summary of
                                            the pressure of simply
                                            speaking, and then,
                                            with a lisp, the
                                            predicament of
                                            meaning.

27   Morns like these – we parted –
1020 Trudging to Eden, looking backward,

420   You'll know it – as you know 'tis Noon –

ESCAPE

463   *I live with Him – I see His face –*

720   *No Prisoner be –*
948   *'Twas Crisis – All the length had passed –*

77   I never hear the word "escape"
867   Escaping backward to perceive
1238 Power is a familiar growth –
1347 Escape is such a thankful Word

1535 The Life that tied too tight escapes
1565 Some Arrows slay but whom they strike –

FOOD

FORGETTING

***

***

FRECKLES

***

***

GRANITE, CRUMBLING

***

***

GOBLIN

***

GOBLIN BEE

***

***

GUEST

HOUSEWIFE

INSOLVENCY, LOSS, GAMBLING, BEGGING

***

MEMORY

***

MOTHER

***

***

***

MUSIC FOR HER FATHER

***

***

261   Put up my lute!
861   Split the Lark – and you'll find the Music –

***

NERVE, NERVES

1046   *I've dropped my Brain – My Soul is numb –*

341   *After great pain, a formal feeling comes –*
497   *He strained my faith –*
1054   *Not to discover weakness is*

244   It is easy to work when the soul is at play –
1128   These are the Nights that Beetles love –

***

NIGHT AND DAY

PEARL

PINK

***

***

***

PLACATING

***

***

223   I came to buy a smile – today –

***

PORTRAITS OF HER FATHER

***

POSTHUMOUS

1489   *A Dimple in the Tomb*

984   *'Tis Anguish grander than Delight*
1529   *'Tis Seasons since the Dimpled War*
1637   *Is it too late to touch you, Dear?*
1643   *Extol thee – could I? Then I will*

1204   Whatever it is – she has tried it –
1205   Immortal is an ample word
1231   Somewhere upon the general Earth
1398   I have no Life but this –
1403   My Maker – let me be
1422   Summer has two Beginnings –
1507   The Pile of Years is not so high
1517   How much of Source escapes with thee –
1525   He lived the Life of Ambush   See also 1616
                                            Oh what a Grace
                                            this is,

1564   Pass to thy Rendezvous of Light,
1594   Immured in Heaven!
1597   'Tis not the swaying frame we miss,
1602   Pursuing you in your transitions,
1625   Back from the cordial Grave I drag thee
1632   So give me back to Death –
1638   Go thy great way!   See also 1525
                                            He lived the Life
                                            of Ambush

1664   I did not reach Thee
1666   I see thee clearer for the Grave   See also 1671
                                             Judgment is justest

1689   The look of thee, what is it like
1699   To do a magnanimous thing
1725   I took one Draught of Life –
1742   The distance that the dead have gone
1743   The grave my little cottage is,
1754   To lose thee – sweeter than to gain

***

POWER, OPPRESSION

PRISON OR IMPRISONMENT

***

ROSE

***

SACRAMENT

SAVIOR, JESUS, CRUCIFIX

SECRET

SEX

SHAME

SIR, MASTER

SIRE

STAB

VOLCANOES

WHEEL

WHITE

WITNESS

RELATIONSHIP TO HIM

***

BIBLIOGRAPHY

Belloc, Hilaire. "The South Country." *An Anthology of Recent Poetry*. L. D'O. Walters, comp. New York: Dodd, Mead And Company, 1920.

Bianchi, Martha Dickinson. *Emily Dickinson Face to Face: Unpublished Letters with Notes and Reminiscences*. Boston and New York: Houghton Mifflin, 1930.

_____. *The Life and Letters of Dickinson*. Boston and New York: Houghton Mifflin, 1930.

Blume, E., Sue. *Secret Survivors: Uncovering Incest and Its Aftereffects in Women*. New York: Ballatine, 1990.

Bly, Robert. *American Poetry, Wildness and Domesticity*. New York: Harper & Row, Publishers, 1990.

Bly, Robert. Woodman, Marion. *The Maiden King: The Reunion of Masculine and Feminine*. New York: Henry Holt, 1998.

Chase, Richard. *Emily Dickinson*. New York: William Sloan Associates, 1951.

Clendenning, Sheila T. *Emily Dickinson. A Bibliography 1850-1966*. Kent State University Press, 1968.

Habegger, Alfred. *My Wars Are Laid Away in Books: The Life of Emily Dickinson*. New York: Random House, 2001.

Hawkes, Jacquetta, ed. *The World of the Past*. New York: Alfred A. Knopf, 1963.

Johnson, Thomas. H., ed. *The Complete Poems of Emily Dickinson*. Boston, New York, London: Little, Brown and Company, 1961.

MacKinnon, Catharine, A. *Only Words*. Cambridge, Massachusetts: Harvard University Press, 1993.

Morison, Samuel Eliot. *The Oxford History of American People*. New York: Oxford University Press, 1965.

Oliner, Samuel, P. and Oliner, Pearl, M. *The Altruistic Personality: Rescuers of Jews in Nazi Occupied Europe*. New York: Free Press, 1988.

Perriman, Wendy, K. *A Wounded Deer: The Effects of Incest on the Life and Poetry of Emily Dickinson*. New Castle, UK: Cambridge Scholars Press, 2006.

Rodgers, Daniel T. *The Work Ethic in Industrial America 1850-1920.* Chicago and London: University of Chicago Press, 1978.

Sewall, Richard B. *The Life of Emily Dickinson*, 2 vols. New York: Farrar, Strauss and Giroux, 1975.

Tindall, George Brown. *America: A Narrative History*, 2 vols. New York, London: W. W. Norton & Company, 1984.

Weil, Monica Lynn. *Inside Incest.* Van Nuys, California: New World Wide Media, 1984.

Uzgalis, William. "John Locke." *The Stanford Encyclopedia of Philosophy*, ed. Edward N. Zalta. http://plato.stanford.edu/archives/win2006/entries/locke/ (accessed May 17, 2007).

Van Doren, Carl. *The Great Rehearsal.* New York: The Viking Press, 1948.

Wainright, William. "Jonathan Edwards." *The Stanford Encyclopedia of Philosophy*, ed. Edward N. Zalta. http://plato.stanford.edu/archives/win2006/entries/edwards/ (accessed May 17, 2007).

Whicher, George Frisbie. *This Was a Poet: A Critical Biography of Emily Dickinson.* New York: Charles Scribner's Sons, 1938.

Wolff, Cynthia Griffin. *Emily Dickinson.* New York: (Radcliffe biography series), Addison-Wesley, 1988.

Woodman, Marion. *Addiction to Perfection, The Still Unravished Bride, A Psychological Study.* Toronto, Canada: Inner City Books, 1982.

Rape Abuse & Incest National Network (RAINN)

Hotline: 1-800-656 HOPE (Counselor, ext.1; donation, ext.2)
www.rainn.org

"If I can stop one Heart from breaking"

Emily Dickinson